THE INSPIRED
WORKSPACE

INTERIOR DESIGNS FOR CREATIVITY & PRODUCTIVITY

GLOUCESTER MASSACHUSETTS

ROCKPORT
PUBLISHERS

MARILYN ZELINSKY

First published in the United States of America by

Rockport Publishers, Inc.

33 Commercial Street

Gloucester, Massachusetts 01930-5089

Telephone: (978) 282-9590

Fax: (978) 283-2742

Library of Congress Cataloging-in-Publication data available

ISBN 1-59253-056-7

10 9 8 7 6 5 4 3 2 1

Cover Design: Bob's Your Uncle

Book Design: Deep Creative

Cover Images: Courtesy of Push

Printed in China

THE INSPIRED
WORKSPACE

ROCKPORT

CONTENTS

"The brain is a wonderful organ; it starts working the moment you get up in the morning and does not stop until you get into the office." Robert Frost, American poet

INTRODUCTION
RECOGNIZING THE INSPIRED WORKSPACE

"Why would we want to spend our days in a dark room without a view? We have enough time for that when we are asleep at night in the darkness of our bedrooms. Our days would be best spent in workspaces that stimulate the senses and envelop us with creative elements in whatever form they take." Marilyn Zelinsky

A friend of mine asked me what I'd learned from writing this book. After all, I'd written about workplace design for years. My answer: "Only brave souls create inspired workspaces." It sounds corny, but it's true. It takes guts to create an inspiring workspace, whether it's an office for one or a corporate campus for hundreds.

I believe that people who buck the trend of bandage-beige cubicles and white walls are true to themselves, to their work, to their employees, and to their workspaces. Only brave people create nap rooms for employees, encourage outside Frisbee games, design offices around their favorite fish, and shape interiors like spaceships or theaters. Though these workspaces may elicit smirks from those who don't work there, critics know deep down that these workspaces are created from passion. They know that anyone who works there is fortunate to be in an exceptional space and part of a rare corporate culture.

Foosball tables, basketball hoops, pool tables, beer taps, or Zen rock gardens—icons like these are really symbols of a company's hope that its employees will loosen up, will find a way to creatively express themselves. What employer wouldn't want that for employees, or themselves, for that matter? Remember the words of a great innovator, IDEO's Tom Kelley. "Finally, don't forget that your spaces should tell stories—about your workers and your company." What story would you like your workspace to say about you and your company? What story does a sterile workspace tell a client or a prospective employee? What story does a nurturing, playful, serene, fantastic, or artistic workspace tell those same people?

This book is not meant to preach a certain design mandate or to sell a specific design solution. The goal of The Inspired Workspace is to provoke thought by presenting design ideas that are all at once personal and cozy, genius and zany. This portfolio of projects shows ways of sensitively handling materials and space that demonstrate the endless possibilities of workspace design that are intended to bring encouragement, comfort, and inspiration to all the people that work, think, and spend many hours there.

Marilyn Zelinsky

"Appealing workplaces are to be avoided. One wants a room with no view, so imagination can meet memory in the dark." Anne Dillard, writer, poet, and environmentalist

"We must learn to be still in the midst of activity and to be vibrantly alive in repose."
Indira Gandhi, political leader of India

Steelcase created a prototype of the ultimate nurturing private office. The Oasis lets employees rest and reflect on their thoughts before returning to the teamwork environment. Steelcase's research points to the need to foster repose as a way to help employees feel innovative and productive.

THE **NURTURING** WORKSPACE

WHERE PEOPLE FEEL COCOONED, COMFORTED, AND CONNECTED

A nurturing workspace exudes comfort and safety. It is a place where employees feel free to unwind and rest and to gather the energy needed to regroup in creative collaboration.

A heightened state of anxiety and activity in the workplace saps people of energy. A culture that encourages employees to acknowledge their need for rest, along with their need for the chaos of collaboration, results in a more joyful workplace where everyone feels safe enough to be who they are and create what they want.

Nurturing workspaces feel almost residential, designed to allow employees to move comfortably throughout the space, making use of the work areas as an employee would in her own home. It's becoming more the norm to find a kitchen, a living room, a library, and even a modified bedroom in today's workplace. While a kitchen in the home is meant for preparing food, one at the workplace is a metaphor for gathering, creating, and sharing an understanding of one another. A living room at home signifies a time to relax, and sofas in the office become the symbols that permit employees to unwind and rest with others while at work. Bedrooms at home symbolize uninterrupted rest; nap areas at work symbolize an acceptance that solitude and siestas are necessary elements to heighten creativity.

The following offices show a mosaic of nurturing workspaces. Massachusetts-based Mariposa features fruity-colored offices and a well-stocked kitchen to help this creative group of employees feel like family. Vitra in Germany opened its walls and furnished its new space with symbols of home to help employees comfortably collaborate, while Gould Evans's Kansas City office offers employees use of "spent tents," as the design firm recognized the need to revive the creative process through shut-eye. Whether it's a corporate office in a large city or a small group of artists in a rural town, the language of comfort is a global one.

BON APPÉTIT!
MARIPOSA

Sometimes, it's the person who has never, ever worked in a typical office who's able to freely design the most inspiring workplace. Livia Cowan, president of Mariposa, a small, but growing tableware company, knows for sure that she would have been fired if she ever worked in a corporate office. Her love of mango-colored walls, disdain for regimentation during the workday, knack for exchanging recipes with coworkers, and need for long lunches with her colleagues would rub a boss's patience the wrong way. But, that's precisely why she's able to attract the best employees for her creative working family.

Mariposa's story started when Cowan was fourteen and bought her first dinnerware set. When Cowan went to college in Mexico, her sister, Deborah, opened Mariposa, a retail store, in Boston. Together, they'd drive back from Mexico in a car loaded with glassware. When her sister closed the store, Cowan took over the wholesale aspect of the business, and ran it from her parents' home in Gloucester. Finally, her parents had enough of Bohemian artisans passing through their house with packs of Mexican glassware. It was time for Mariposa to mature; after all, it was selling goods to Neiman Marcus, Bergdorf Goodman, and Gumps.

After searching for an industrial space to house Mariposa, Cowan found The Barn on Elm Street (often referred to as the "nightmare on Elm Street" after she purchased it). The dilapidated, turn-of-the-century structure had served for years as the livery stable for the town of Manchester, and was later the headquarters to an exterminating company. The future headquarters of Mariposa was filled with old tractors, a Studebaker, other cars used for parts, and the 1960s exterior Christmas decorations from the Jordan Marsh store at the local mall. In short, it was a pit, Cowan says. But it was sturdy, had character, and would serve its purpose. Cowan worked with the architecture firm of Olson Lewis & Dioli Architects & Planners to create one of the most inspiring workplaces in town.

During the summer, the hayloft doors on the backside of the second story are left open for cross ventilation. Employees often meet, read, or lunch outside at the granite table alongside the inlet that borders the property. The landscaping is planted with soft and indigenous lilacs, blueberries, and Rosa rugosa. Michael Updike, who designs Mariposa's aluminum serve ware, designed a sculpture for the backyard.

Everyone takes turns preparing a meal, so only one person is in the kitchen at a time. And the copy machine gets a good workout from employees duplicating recipes for one another. "It creates a sense of community and family," Cowan says. The kitchen's colors—curry and mandarin—provide an appetizing backdrop for meetings and luncheons. The yellow softens the dramatic effect of the red and creates a soothing, yet energizing, space. Glass-paned, lighted cabinets allow Mariposa's product lines to shine.

> "I see a big difference in behavior between a formal meeting and a lunch. People are more open and willing to chat over food." Livia Cowan, president, Mariposa

A WORKSPACE LIKE HOME

Out of this nightmare came a workplace that could easily be called a home: a nurturing, light-filled, color-infused office space where laughter can commonly be heard and gourmet food can always be found.

The two-story barn is divided up with offices for fourteen employees on the second floor and a kitchen, known as the cornerstone of the headquarters. (Another seven employees work at the company's distribution center.) The large, well-equipped kitchen was essential to Cowan, because each member of the company loves to cook, eat, and present food to one another. Mariposa attracts those who appreciate not only the product lines, but also the gourmand's lifestyle both during and after work.

As soon as the barn could be occupied, the colleagues began to make gourmet lunches for each other and the construction crew. The lucky crew lowered their scaffolding down one day to the lower level where they were served fresh haddock, ratatouille, and pilaf right through the window.

But there's more to these lunches than just the downtime and the good food. Cowan says that cooking and dining together has the same effect as the traditional Sunday dinner for a family where you catch up with each other and take the time to understand what's going on in each other's lives. And, it gives the group a chance to follow up on conversation about work. Great new product ideas—from new designs to new lines—come out of these lunches, Cowan says.

> "Providing a comfortable, inspiring environment shows respect for my co-workers. In turn, they naturally gather enthusiasm for the products and every aspect of the business... a feeling that emanates to the larger business community."
>
> Livia Cowan, president, Mariposa

ATTRACTING EMPLOYEES

Cowan says she draws quality employees to Mariposa because of the food and the open atmosphere. She's constantly receiving resumes because people hear Mariposa is a great place to work. The downside of a creative workspace like Mariposa? In all her years, Cowan has had one employee who could not handle the casual, family-style atmosphere. Though the employee loved the workspace, she felt rudderless and closed up in Mariposa's entrepreneurial environment. That employee quickly found a job at a large sneaker manufacturer that provided more structure. On other occasions, lack of cooking skills embarrasses employees who aren't gourmet cooks, but they quickly realize it's easy to make a simple meal.

Do employees abuse the freedoms of such a nurturing workspace? Cowan says each employee is grateful for the open environment. Moms run out to school plays, people pop on home to walk the dog or whatever needs to be done during the day. But each person is responsible and makes up the time in order to get the work done.

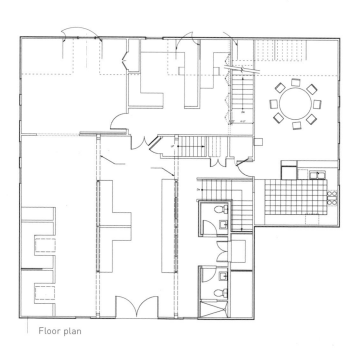

Floor plan

Office workstations are crafted in tongue-in-groove woodwork with mandarin-colored Formica work surfaces. The 46-inch-high (1,150 centimeter-high) panels offer privacy, but are low enough for open exchange among employees. The crew gathers to work on new product lines near the kitchen in a conference room (called the living room). The customer service area features walls painted the color of yellow tulips.

True, people with allergies to animals, who fear fleas, who don't care for cats or dogs, and don't much appreciate the smell of wet fur and bone breath, may not like the idea of pets in the workplace. But for the majority of workers, seeing furry friends in the office provides a breath of fresh air and acts as a calming force to focus on during the workday.

More studies show that pets reduce stress in the workplace. In a survey of 193 employees in thirty-one Kentucky companies polled by Eastern Kentucky University professors Dr. Meredith Wells and Dr. Rose Perrine, businesses that allowed pets tend to be smaller in size. The survey published in the *Journal of Occupational Health Psychology* (2001) reported that only a minority of employees found it troublesome to encounter noise from barking, hair on furniture, and symptoms from allergies. In addition, most employees reported that pets in the workplace fostered social interaction and are good for business.

ANIMALS INSPIRE CREATIVITY

A national study by the American Pet Products Manufacturers Association found that 100 percent of the companies it polled agreed that having pets in the workplace relaxes employees.

- 73 percent of the companies surveyed said that having pets in the workplace leads to a more creative environment.
- None of the companies with pets in the office said they had an increased absenteeism rate and 27 percent of the respondents had a decreased absenteeism rate.
- 73 percent of companies with pets in the office said that pets help build employee relations and helped to improve interpersonal skills.
- 56 percent of offices with pets say that their employees are willing to work overtime.
- 92 percent of companies with pets in the office say that less than 25 percent of employees smoke.

MARIPOSA'S MASCOT

How do Mariposa employees feel about having Lola around all day? "She has a wonderful calming effect on all of us in the office," Cowan says. Lola sits in the chair opposite Cowan's desk during the day, as if she's interviewing for a job at Mariposa. Each morning, Lola greets the customer service team, and everyone gets to start the day off with a good laugh while looking at the adorable, scruffy face. Says Cowan, "Best is when stuffy accountant-types arrive in suit, acting really professional... and she suddenly makes them laugh!"

Lola, the office's Portuguese water dog and mascot, brings joy to Mariposa's fourteen employees during the workday.

Once upon a time, the two-hour lunch was a staple of the workplace. According to a survey by Steelcase, a leading office furniture manufacturer, even the typical one-hour lunch is a now thing of the past. Results show that 40 percent of 1,000 people interviewed in the United States said they use their lunch hour to catch up on work at their desks rather than taking the time to socialize or run errands.

A healthy 38 percent of those surveyed, however, still enjoy eating lunch with colleagues and co-workers. Why? Because breaking bread with co-workers gives them a feeling of community and enhanced understanding amongst one another that is often lost during the workday, especially in more traditional hierarchical offices.

"Isolation in creative work is an onerous thing. Better to have negative criticism than nothing at all." Anton Chekhov, Russian writer, and physician

BREATHING ROOM
VITRA

Vitra, known for its cutting-edge office furniture used in workplaces worldwide, faced a need to redesign its own 120-employee workplace in Germany, at the Weil am Rhein complex. The 7,382-square-foot (2,250-square-meter) office occupies the mezzanine floor of one of the company's factory buildings, which was designed in 1984 by English architect Nicholas Grimshaw & Partners. Before London-based architect Sevil Peach Gence Associates redesigned the space, offices were confined to a small area of the footprint, while the dark, isolated back section of the building served as showroom and storage area.

The company decided not only to redesign the space but also to restructure the departments, moving client-oriented divisions together to form a single unit. The idea was to create an open, fluid, and flexible office environment that would help employees feel at ease both with the space and with each other. But to give employees true freedom, the office design lets workers choose from an abundance of workspaces that correspond to their own needs—from the café to break areas, group rooms, and meeting zones. Unlike workplaces with fixed desks and offices, Vitra's employees are encouraged to move freely throughout the rooms of the workspace as they would in their own homes. There are only two closed rooms—one for human resources and one for the managing director of the office.

DESIGNING A REFUGE

The first step involved in opening up the entire interior envelope was to strip the existing interior, revealing the building's basic structure of concrete beams, pillars, and a metal roof deck and concrete floor. This new and fresh empty canvas of space allowed the architects to divide the interior. Now, there are defined zones of eighty-seven workplaces divided into territorial and nonterritorial spaces, areas for communication and concentration. Some of the staff visit the office only to attend meetings. This group can use project rooms, larger meeting areas, benches, sofas, and the café for spontaneous meetings.

Here is a view from the library's ocular window into the warmly lit conference room.

Blond birch plywood walls and built-in shelves line the research library. The hushed area is filled with literature and magazines to help employees catch up on the design industry. Comfortable cushioned seating and soft lighting give the space a relaxed and residential feeling.

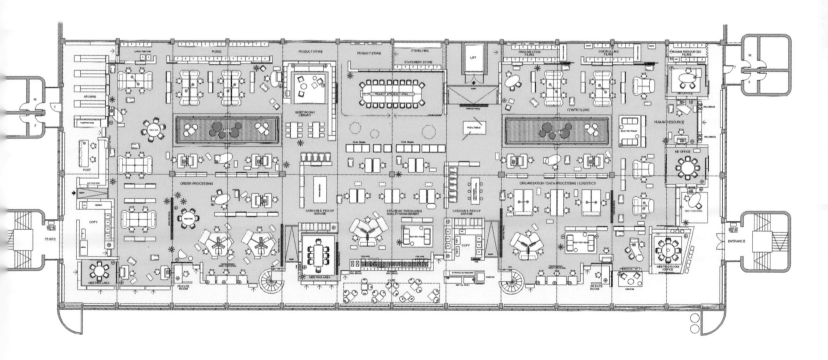

"The society based on production is only productive, not creative." Albert Camus, French writer and philosopher

The raised, freestanding platform is a symbolic and partial separation between dedicated work areas and shared spaces such as the café, post area, technical rooms, and the access route.

Special spaces welcome employees who drop into the office for meetings. The project room holds up to twenty-four people and can be sectioned off with a curtain. Natural light from large windows streams in to warm up living room–style meeting areas.

Large, movable canvas panels hang from concrete beams by ultra-sturdy cargo straps. Not only do panels double as notice boards and projection areas, they also contribute to acoustics.

SPECS

HALLMARKS OF MODERN RESIDENTIAL-STYLE WORKSPACE

- floor lamps with shades
- wood-paneled walls
- upholstered sofas
- hanging fabrics and curtains to divide work areas
- mailbox in-boxes
- raised wood platform floors
- birch plywood walls

"People get more done when they can sleep." Bob Gould, architect

BATTLING FATIGUE
GOULD EVANS'S WESTPORT CENTER

Ever wonder why the idea of taking an afternoon siesta never caught on in the typical office setting? In the recent past, most employees caught snoozing at work—behind closed office doors, in bathroom stalls, in quiet, dark conference rooms—were labeled plain lazy. But what if it was okay to take a catnap on company time? Gould Evans, an architectural and design company headquartered in Kansas City, decided to take the stigma out of napping after an executive member of the firm was seen slumped over his desk, exhausted from working long hours on an important project. Instead of getting angry, the firm got smart, and erected what they call "spent tents" for drained employees in need of a nurturing nap.

The napping area was ultimately integrated into the office space, a converted retail store in a minimall. The firm had chosen 30,000 square feet (2,787 square meters) to convert into a technologically advanced workplace with the amenities of home. The goal was to redesign the space at $50 a square foot. It was a design process of experimentation and collaboration between associates and management.

NAPPING NOW ALLOWED

The office is casual and people-friendly with open office spaces to foster teaming for the 150-plus associates at this site. Along with lots of natural daylight and low-cost, non-fussy materials are napping tents. The tents, a way to test increasing productivity during project deadlines, were the brainchild of Bob Gould, principal, and Karen Gould, interior designer at the firm.

Designers are often notorious for keeping odd and long hours, especially when demanding clients and deadlines are always a problem. The designers at Gould Evans got the idea for sleeping tents when they realized the only way to retain and attract top talent was to make them happy and comfortable during arduous project work when everyone had to gather together for long hours. The tents have remained up and active for a few years. Associates use the tents when they work long or strange hours, as a type of infirmary when they aren't feeling well, an area to kick back and relax to regroup, a place for nursing mothers to have some privacy. In addition, they are intriguing to clients. "Clients want to come to our office for meetings, when in the neighborhood, and just to see what's next," says Karen Gould.

Each of the three spent tents has a sleeping bag, pillow, camping mat, eyeshade, alarm clock, and Walkman equipped with relaxation music. The tent is set up in a private area of the office underneath an airflow system that creates lots of white noise.

Flexibility is a key theme at Gould Evans's Kansas City office. Not only are employees allowed to snooze in pup tents, but they are free to arrange mobile office furniture on a whim.

According to a recent survey by William A. Anthony, director of Boston University's Center for Psychiatric Rehabilitation, and author of *The Art of Napping at Work* (Larson Publications, 1999), 70 percent of 1,000 respondents said they nap at work. People squirrel away five to ten minutes of rest at their desk, in their car, bathroom, or in another locked room on the premises, according to Anthony. He advises companies to encourage napping during lunch, or instituting breaks when employees are able to snooze to bring their energy back to optimum levels.

Luckily, there's no need to nap during the day for much longer than fifteen to twenty minutes, says James Maas, a Cornell University psychologist who offers "Power Sleep" seminars to large companies. The need to nap is particularly strong roughly eight hours after you wake, Maas says, because that's when we tend to have a huge dip in how alert we are. A short nap helps us regain creativity and problem-solving skills.

FORTY WINKS AT WORK

History loves a napper. Thomas Jefferson, a serious napper, had an office complete with bed and pillow. Napping on the job lost its luster after Jefferson, and became the secret of innovative, productive home-based workers everywhere. Today, employers concerned about sleep-deprived employees are slowly allowing workers to recharge their batteries.

The benefits can't be disputed. According to a National Sleep Foundation poll, sleep deprivation continues to be widespread—63 percent of American adults do not get enough sleep. There's a direct relationship to hours worked and its negative impact on sleep, the foundation maintains. Over half the workforce reports that sleepiness on the job interferes with the amount of work done, and diminishes the quality and quantity by 30 percent. Most adults, the foundation found, would gladly nap at work if their employers allowed them to.

The police department in Albuquerque took this problem to heart. It formed a program aimed at reducing sleep deprivation among its officers because the problem was becoming one that compromised public safety. Tired cops drove when drowsy, reacted to more minor irritations, and had trouble remembering things. To enhance alertness, a few major reforms were put in place, including a sixty-hour cap on the number of hours officers work in a given week. Time sheets were redesigned to better log an officer's time.

"For fast acting relief, try slowing down." Lily Tomlin, comedian

Thomas Jefferson, a notorious napper, was fond of catching some shut-eye in his cabinet during the workday.

Twenty-five years ago, Craig Yarde, Senior, started his metal working company from his basement. He fed coworkers homemade food and wine during the day and free beer at day's end, and everyone became more like family than employees. Suddenly, Yarde hired 100 people in one year, but with no organizational plan, no experience working in a traditional office, and no charts to guide him. Yarde simply let his instincts lead him to hire the best people by paying high, expecting hard work, and giving back to each employee a bonus based on the company's earnings. Unfortunately, workers had an inflated idea of what Yarde Metals earned, and resented the bonuses because they thought they were too low.

Yarde realized his employees didn't trust him and decided to open the company's books to everyone. Now, all 450 associates in every branch and on every shift are taught and required to know how to read a balance sheet to understand the fair distribution of profits. "Everyone has perspective and there are no surprises about how the company is doing," Yarde says. "They know the good and the bad."

NURTURING METALWORKERS

The extraordinary nurturing workplace environment Yarde created continues to draw attention, and that, too, is evolving. The Yarde Metals facility in Bristol, Connecticut, is the home of the original nap room that garnered attention in the press in the 1990s. "I just legalized what everyone was doing," Yarde says about the associates who used to nap on their desk for twenty minutes. To this day, the company celebrates "National Workplace Nap Day," and Yarde encourages workers to come to the party in their most creative nap outfits (including curlers and slippers). Even the small New Hampshire branch of twenty people has a nap room, in addition to an emergency daycare room, a dog kennel, antique furniture, and stained glass personally chosen by Yarde.

But the 60,000-square-foot (5,574-square-meter) building in Bristol is too small for this growing company. A half-million-square-foot (45,000-square-meter) state-of-the-art facility is being built in nearby Southington, Connecticut. "The metal industry is known as a greasy, dirty place," Yarde says. "I want to bring the industry out of the 1800s and lift up its image."

The new facility will have five dog kennels with runs out back, an outside picnic area, bocce ball and basketball courts, two nap rooms, a game room, huge fountains and seating areas, Victorian street lights throughout the interior, a minimuseum for the metal industry, and a small retail store where Yarde will sell its imported virgin olive oil and Yarde Mountain Coffee Company beans. Proceeds from the sales go towards scholarships for the employees' families. There will also be a room to store Yarde's collection of 5,000 *Life* magazines that he gives away to vendors and customers on birthdays, providing he has an issue with the corresponding year. But the crown jewel of the space will no doubt be the conference room table that will be fashioned from the company's original delivery truck, a 1963 Diamond Reo that has been restored and turned into a table base.

It's not unusual to find a Yarde Metals employee wearing slippers! Yarde has received national attention for its innovative idea of letting employees nap during work hours. After reading that sleep deprivation poses problems for 2nd and 3rd shift workers, the company contacted Bill and Camille Anthony, authors of *The Art of Napping*, and with their help instituted an open nap policy.

"Write down the thoughts of the moment. Those that come unsought for are commonly the most valuable." Francis Bacon, author

A VERTICAL VILLAGE
CAMPUS MLC/LEND LEASE

MLC, the financial-services arm of Lend Lease, a global real-estate management firm, may have stayed over the years in the original building built in 1957, but its workforce has sure changed since then, and their offices in North Sydney, Australia, reflect these changes. Back in the 1950s, nearly all the employees were corporate men in dark gray flannel suits. Today, MLC calculates that about 70 percent of its workforce are considered to be Generation X, the under–forty crowd. It became clear that the workspace had to transform itself to keep up with the fresh faces of MLC and the new, larger-scope business mandate of the global real estate company.

A tropical fish tank occupies the far end of the Zen Den. Behind the tank is a table that employees have to climb on in order to sit on it. To use the white board, you have to climb onto the table.

Go down the stairs and enter level three, named the Zen Den, where there are giant amoebic sofas and dishes filled with stones that employees can play with to relieve stress or use to stand around and ponder an idea.

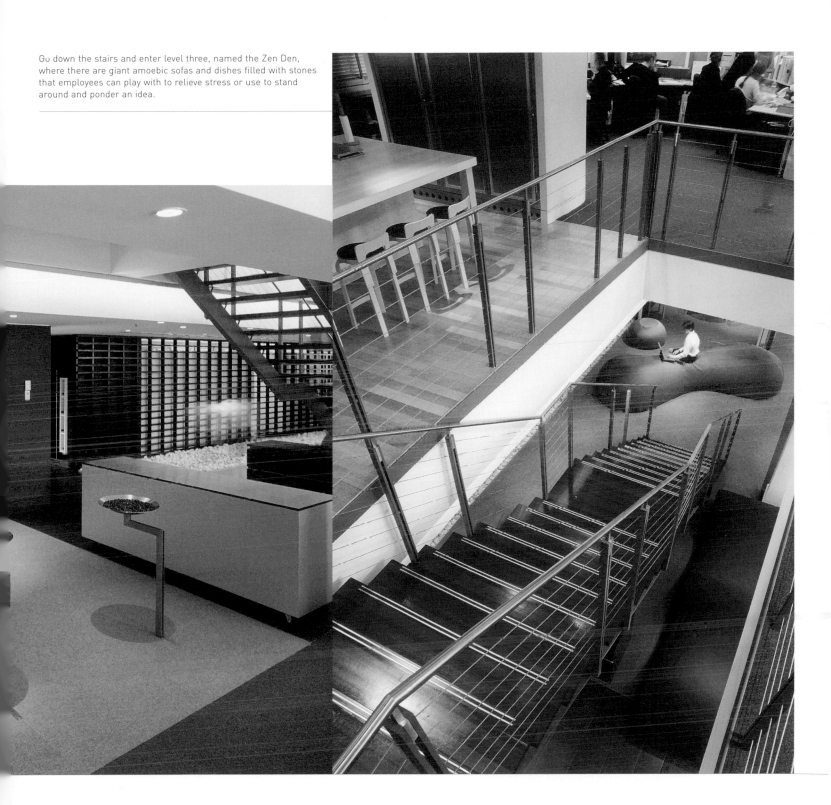

"My ideas usually come not at my desk writing but in the midst of living." Anaïs Nin, author

A NEW VISION

The task was to design a place to meet and nurture one another, versus a place to merely work together. Rosemary Kirkby, MLC's general staff manager, spearheaded the change of workspace to match the change of workplace—one that had moved from a severe hierarchy into a more flat structure of teams and business units. Kirkby corralled architects DEGW of Sydney to provide programming data, and hired architect James Grose, of Bligh Voller Nield, who specializes in residential design. Kirkby's intention was that Grose would bring a new vision to what a corporate interior should look and act like.

It began with a word. Kirkby wasn't sure what the new space should look like, but she began by writing the word "imagine" on a piece of paper. From there, she brainstormed and realized what was percolating in her mind. She wanted to "imagine" what it would be like to work for a company that did everything in its power to make the workplace energizing, inspirational, nurturing, and exciting. Kirkby wanted to create a campus so those ten hours an employee dedicated to the company could be the best hours of their day. But what would that workspace actually look like?

A small meeting room dubbed "the hospital curtain" area is a private place to escape.

One elevator lobby is painted with chalkboard paint—walls filled with graffiti mark the ideas and complaints of the day.

WHAT YOUNG WORKERS WANT

What Kirkby and Grose determined was that the young crowd at MLC did not view work as stable career, but as a static lifestyle where boundaries blur and mesh, then separate again at different times of the day, week, or month. Kirkby and Grose wanted to create an interior where an employee would stay at MLC because of the comfort and flexibility of the workspace, rather than flee to the competition for a few thousand dollars more in salary.

The response was to at first create an open stair that would cut through eleven existing floors to create a vertical pedestrian street. Then, each floor was given a different theme with furniture and finishes that matched accordingly. One floor, with blue and yellow striped carpet, is called The Beach. The Zen Den on level three features tatami mats and bamboo sculptures. The Table on level four has a kitchen and long communal table for meals or meetings. The eighth floor features the Forum, a theater-in-the-round for lounging and for large-scale company meetings.

Individual workspaces are not forgotten in favor of fun and deliberate common spaces. There are no dedicated private offices, only fully adjustable workstations attached to posts that are hot-wired. Even the CEO does not have a private office. Corners of the building are occupied not by executive offices but by project and meeting rooms. Finally, no one owns a window workstation. If someone wants a quiet moment or a view outside, there are plenty of silent pods and quiet rooms with windows for private phone conferences.

As a result of the refurbishing and reprogramming of workspaces, Kirkby gained two extra floors of office space, which translated into a 33 percent saving in workspace. And that's more than enough to handle the company's future growth, while adding a few more inspired theme spaces along the way.

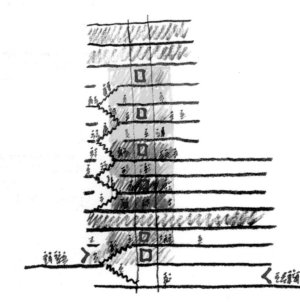

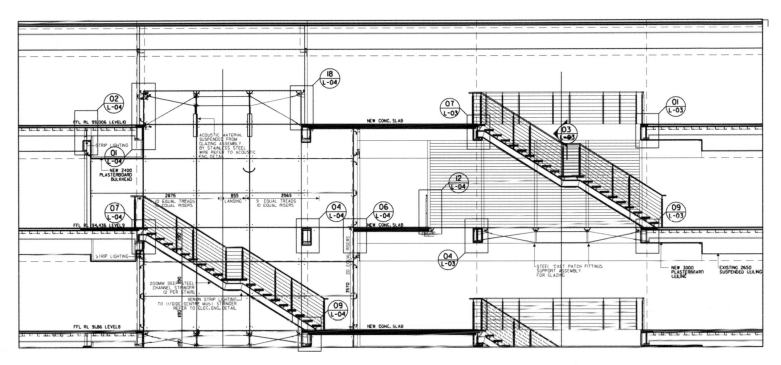

05 STAIR SECTION 1:50
‾‾ LEVELS 8,9 & 10

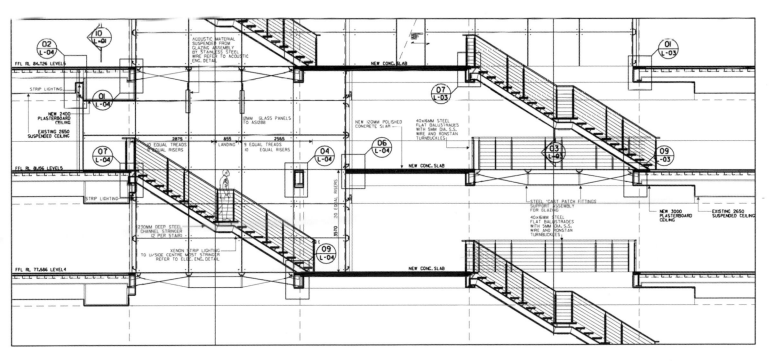

06 STAIR SECTION 1:50
‾‾ LEVELS 4,5 & 6

> **"The analysis of data will not by itself produce new ideas."**
> Edward de Bono, author, creative-thinking teacher and expert

NESTING PLACE
ACCENTURE

"At Accenture, we are not just employees, but individuals with our own unique needs," says Trisha Dickie, director of facilities and services, local technology support. Accenture follows through on that belief by providing a comfortable, nurturing, yet productive workspace for the employees of this leading global management and technology consulting services organization.

"Travel is a way of life for many Accenture employees, so we wanted to create a comfortable environment for them at the office," Dickie says. "We did not want to create a formal or 'rigid' environment." The objective of this 160,000 square-foot (14,865-square-meter) three-and-a-half-floor space in Ontario was to turn the traditional concept of a workspace on its ear, creating a nurturing office and landing place for hardworking traveling employees.

Dickey called in design firm Marshall Cummings to create this type of work environment. "Our global model for our offices is 'hoteling,' and we wanted to bring in an extra layer of comfort to the office space," she says.

FOUR-SEASON WORKSPACE

The hoteling part was easy to program; each enclosed space is universal in size, there are huddle rooms and telephone booths for private conversations. The main challenge was in creating a professional, yet inspired atmosphere.

"I can't think of a more effective or more inspiring theme for an office space than the four seasons," Dickie says.

Heppner created a hoteling space that provides a number of workstation options that can be reserved in advance. Herman Miller's Resolve systems are used throughout the space. When Dickie first saw Resolve, she wasn't convinced it would work in the space. But she says she gets more requests from employees to reserve Resolve workstations than she anticipated. "People really prefer social environments, and that's what this system provides," Dickie says.

A FIRST-RATE HOTEL

Other hoteling spaces range from "focus rooms," private offices, open spaces, team, and more collaborative project rooms. The typical Accenture employee is a microcosm of the rest of the corporate world in that the employee won't spend the whole day in one central location, but instead will move around to an appropriate setting where and when the work requires.

One of the most inspired parts of the office space, Dickie says, is the way the natural daylight is used. "Our employees really enjoy the natural light," she says. "The four walls of our building are windows so there's no blockage to the natural daylight as it shines through."

Here, the spring quadrant of the Accenture workspace has Herman Miller Resolve screens that are tinted with stripes of fresh green to mimic imagery of nature's new growth. It's one of the ways the designers captured Canada's four seasons in the workspace.

Rough stone cladding, a Muskoka trademark, can be seen throughout the workspace. The downstairs lounge features a beautiful fireplace with stone cladding, a great getaway space from daily activity. Another lounge called The Dock opens with large wood-paneled doors into a room with a wood-burning fireplace and authentic Muskoka chairs, which create a cozy place for fireside meetings and chats. Erik Heppner, who led the design team, brought a photo of a rustic Muskoka-style living room to one of the first client presentation meetings to illustrate the mood he had in mind for the space. The Muskokas are made up of lakes in central and northern Ontario. This region has exhilarating landscapes including lakes, forest, ragged shorelines, and granite cliffs bathed by the sun. Accenture loved the concept and from there Heppner designed a few corporate home-style lounges in the Muskoka style.

"The light shines right through the entire space, which creates a wonderful 'lift' for everyone who works here." Trisha Dickie, Accenture

The lobby and elevator are painted a rich Indian red typical of a Canadian cottage-country home found on a rustic lake. According to Algonquin native language, Muskoka is loosely translated as "the land of red earth." The flooring combines wood and rough stone, natural materials meant to give employees a sense of home and comfort. "Our employees have to constantly adapt to changing market conditions very quickly," says Trisha Dickie, director, facilities and services, Accenture, Canada. Earth tones and comfortable surroundings are a way to create a positive working environment," Dickie adds.

"There is nothing so wasteful as doing with great efficiency that which doesn't have to be done at all." Anonymous

THE SOUND OF SILENCE
ORANGE CALL CENTER

Is there such a thing as a peaceful call center? You wouldn't think so. Typically, call centers are environments filled with fleeting employees and are more like stress stations, cauldrons of space filled with noise, not calm. One call center in Darlington, England, defies that stereotype. It is bright and cheery—and tranquil besides. How did Nicholas Grimshaw & Partners (NGP) create an inspirational, quality, and above all, quiet call center for Orange, the U.K.'s wireless-service giant?

CREATING A HUSH

Architect Simon Beames of NGP found this space in Nexus, a 63,000-square-foot (5,853-square-meter) building outside Darlington, in northeast England. Nexus is a simple building, but Beames worked on the interior to create a stress-free workspace for 450 operators who answer 250,000 customer-service calls weekly.

Keen to ensure a hospitable internal environment and enhanced quality of personal workspace, Beames used much of the budget for the interior spaces. The workspaces are open plan and double height to give the employees more breathing room. Rising above the main room is the mezzanine with kitchen. Workspaces are lightweight and simple in design, because at the drop of a hat, the office building may need to turn the space right back into a warehouse due to fluctuating economic conditions. It was quite a puzzle for Beames to solve. Yet by focusing on lighting and sound considerations for the comfort of the employees—and not fussing with furniture and interior accessories—each condition was met.

SOOTHING LIGHTING

The lighting tree petals were born out of the need to support but temper a built-in roof level lighting system. The petals reflect rays from column-mounted uplighters while at the same time diffuse the sunlight streaming through 6-meter (19.7-foot) ETFE (strong, transparent, lightweight material) foil circular roof lights. Floating kite-like in the upper reaches of the building, the petals create a striking visual impression, promoting an image of the building (and its client) as unique and dynamic, qualities not readily associated with a low-budget, industrial structure that houses a call center.

When the south bank of shades are raised, the public has the opportunity to see into the mechanics of the call center, a metaphor to promote the approachability of this modern company who touts round-the-clock service.

Though the space is open wide, noise levels rarely exceed thirty decibels, the sound of a whisper. The wall surface is half perforated, then lined with 6 inches (152 millimeters) of insulation. A bank of wood storage closets warms up the space. The kitchen on the mezzanine has a glass façade, so the kitchen employees feel like they are part of Orange's call center team.

"An idea can turn to dust or magic, depending on the talent that rubs against it."
Bill Bernbach, advertising executive

The call center does not lack for light. The 198-foot-long by 30-foot-high (60-meter long by 9.1-meter high) window wall along the south elevation provides natural light and an excellent view out over the newly landscaped campus.

Unusual petal-shaped light diffusers keep the workspace cool, but well-lighted. Petals, each one 12-feet wide (3.65-meters) tilt to redistribute light when necassary. Lights come from 10 1,000 watt overhead lamps diffused by the elegant petals.

"When they are alone they want to be with others, and when they are with others they want to be alone. After all, human beings are like that." Gertrude Stein, author

In a post-occupancy study, every executive cited as one of their favorite and positive spaces the restaurant-like coffee bar. At first, staff thought using the café would be viewed as wasted time, but its informality and liveliness became a magnet for small meetings with clients and each other.

The Parlor Room is accessible from the lobby. Tour groups use the room as a home base for their belongings and to rest. It's residential in feel with large sofas, bookcases, floor pillows, and knickknacks to set the mood for the tour and to help guests relax.

EXECUTIVE HOMESTEAD
HERMAN MILLER SENIOR LEADERSHIP SPACE

One day Michael Volkema, CEO of Herman Miller, realized the senior leaders of this cutting-edge office furniture company still worked in traditional private executive office suites located at various sites throughout this corporation's facility in West Michigan. Volkema realized it was time to gather the team in a single space for better and faster communication that would lead to quicker decision-making in the development of new products. What better place to co-locate but in the company's famed Design Yard, the company's R&D facility where new products were born and clients were given tours. It was here that Volkema envisioned a place where the executive team would instantaneously connect with not only each other, but also with touring architects, designers, and facility professionals.

BEING NEIGHBORLY

Meyer, Scherer & Rockcastle, the Minneapolis-based firm that created the original Design Yard in 1987, was called in to reconfigure the space. The design team, headed by Lynn Barnhouse of MS&R, held visioning sessions with the executives to understand their needs and wants, keeping in mind that this was the place where clients would come to meet the president of Herman Miller. In other words, the design could not be ostentatious but should embody and support the spirit of flexible workplaces that Herman Miller's products advocate.

The concept of "front doors" and "backyards" evolved. Front doors give clients access to the fourteen executives that co-located, but backyards let executives meet, relax, and concentrate in private backyards away from the tour groups. The rule is that neighbors share backyards, but customers can't be invited into that space because it is specifically there as a sanctuary for the executives to use.

It was the best way to accommodate the executive team's needs, wants, but also their fears, Barnhouse says. "They knew and wanted to get out of their private offices, but there was a fear factor. Yet, they originally wanted to work in Resolve, a new open workstation product from Herman Miller," she says. "But it was far too exposed for them, so we customized Ethospace so workstations would have tent tops and doors."

Profound changes immediately began to occur. "I heard comments that there's no longer a problem with 'schedule tag.' It doesn't take the executives three days to schedule a meeting anymore," Barnhouse says. "And though they struggled with the fear of leaving private offices and teams of people for what they thought would be a dark, dank workspace, the executives all say they can't imagine working anyplace else."

AN OFFICE BECOMES A HOME

In fact, the executives realized they could have fun with their spaces. One executive with extensive international travel experience and a collection of global artifacts set up Chinese pots and an African stool to express his passions. "The workspace looked residential," Barnhouse says. "It helped everyone else to see that it was okay to create a workspace that helped show that a genuine person lived there."

The move paid off. The executive team has improved their day-to-day knowledge of new product initiatives that take place in the Design Yard. The awareness of future products comes up even more in their daily conversations, and they've increased their sensitivity to design details and their understanding and expectations of how a product performs. But the best sign that the co-location is a success? Several executives remarked that after being secluded in subdued private office suites before the move, it's comforting and nurturing to hear laughter coming from a colleague in the backyard.

"'Brave New Work' isn't about grand visions or leaping into tomorrow; it's about having the courage to take chances and the integrity to learn from the results."

Michael Schrage, author and co-director of MIT Media Lab initiatives

Five private "backyards" of about 500 square feet (46.45 square meters) are accessible from executive offices of 112 square feet (10.4 square meters). Backyards are meeting spaces, unwinding areas. Each office has a different quality but captures the essence of a nurturing home: one feels more kitchen-like, one is more like a library, the other more like a family room with couches and other soft seating.

"It's fun doing the impossible."
Walt Disney, pioneer in animated cartoons and founder of Disneyland

THE FANTASY
WORKSPACE

WHERE PEOPLE FEEL TRANSFORMED IN TIME, SPACE, AND PLACE

The fantasy workspace is designed to transform employees from one world into the next as they leave behind the day-to-day surroundings. They can then act out their roles in creative and unique ways.

What exactly does a fantasy workspace do for creativity? Innovative companies know that exceptional success is linked to the unexpected, yet thrilling experiences that a shopper, a client, or an employee has while inside a controlled environment. A fantasy workspace sets a stage for this. Companies that like to invent fantasy workspaces know they are creating an environment that takes the employee out of the ordinary and into a dream world.

Think about the most mundane office space; then, daydream about what you'd like it to look like. How would you feel in your fantasy workspace? Inspired? Relaxed? Excited? That's the power of working in a place that looks like it fell out of your daydreams. Think theme parks, think the magic of Disney World. It's the stuff dreams are made of.

The following workspaces bring fantasy into the everyday workday. The workspace of Duffy Design, a graphics company located in New York City, looks anything but what you'd expect a Manhattan office to look like. Instead, employees exit the elevator into an environment that looks more like an elegant spaceship ready for takeoff, quite a metaphor for a company on the cutting-edge of design. Herman Miller transformed its showroom in Chicago into a color-infused fantasyland, hard to do in a space that is meant to show off office furniture to potential clients.

But it changed plain vanilla white walls into a fantastical light show by the use of strong lighting effects. And who could not resist a loft in Paris, an ideal work/live situation we can only dream of owning. The homeowner is lucky enough to live in a magical city, but also works in a breathtaking light-infused space, complete with pool and gym, which is shared with visiting clients, as well.

It really doesn't matter where in the world these fantasy workspaces are located; it's the experience of what's inside that counts for all who work there.

"Without this playing with fantasy no creative work has ever yet come to birth. The debt we owe to the play of imagination is incalculable."
Carl Jung, psychologist and psychiatrist

"When you come to a roadblock, take a detour."
Mary Kay Ash, entrepreneur and founder of Mary Kay Cosmetics

ROAD TRIP
GOULD EVANS'S STUDIO AT THIRD AVENUE

Gould Evans found their new offices in a characterless building from the 1960s, but quickly turned the 7,000 square-foot (650.3-square-meter) building into an inspiring workspace "on the move." Principals Trudi Hummel, Jay Silverberg, and Bob Gould stripped down the interior of the building to reveal the well-built bones, which would soon become a backdrop for the experimental workplace the principals envisioned.

The open studio is designed to support Gould Evans's teamwork-based approach to design and client service. There are virtually no walls in the space, and teams can be reconfigured instantaneously because all the furniture is on wheels. For instance, it took just four hours to reconfigure twenty-seven people from multiple teams. Typically, that could take weeks and cost a great deal in materials and labor.

Although mobile desks are ideal here, the team realized a private place was needed for meetings. The solution: a vintage 8-foot-wide by 24-foot-long by 8-foot-high (2.4-meter-wide by 7.3-meter-long by 2.4-meter-high) meter) Airstream trailer purchased from someone's backyard in North Kansas City. The 1945 classic was gutted, outfitted, polished, re-wired, and then driven to Kansas and right into the office space. There's nothing like a leisurely jaunt in a trailer to stir up a little creativity.

A few details of this vintage 24-foot-long (7.3-meter-long) Airsteam were left alone. Drawings are clipped to original curtain rods, and the taillights turn into nightlights that light up the front windows of the office space.

Gould Evans moved into a nondescript 1960s building. Once inside, everything is on wheels, from furniture to the once-rolling Airstream conference room. The nostalgic Airstream seems to embody the bohemian spirit of the era during which the office space was built.

FAMOUS AIRSTREAMS

Vintage Airstreams are now considered to be a unique brand of architecture, used as studios, darkrooms, editing suites, offices, waiting rooms, and guest rooms.

- Neiman Marcus's 1996 Christmas catalog offered a vintage Airstream trailer with a fantasy interior and a gold-plated price tag of $195,000.
- Hollywood actors love vintage Airstreams. Famous owners include Tom Hanks, Anthony Edwards, Sean Penn, David Duchovny, Matthew Modine, and Jack Nicholson.
- MTV installed a 1957 model as a waiting room in its Santa Monica headquarters.

Douglas Keister, co-author of *Ready to Roll*, a book about Airstream owners and their lifestyles, shot this trailer court, where only vintage-trailer owners are allowed to park.

SPECS
LEISURE SUITE

An Airstream trailer over twenty years old is considered to be vintage. When the Airstream Trailer Company introduced the Clipper model in 1936, the riveted aluminum body looked more like an aircraft than an automobile. Inside, it slept four, had an enclosed galley, and was fitted with electric lights. It even offered air conditioning through a system that used dry ice. At $1,200, the Clipper was considered expensive, but the orders poured in. Today, there's an influx of requests for those old and dusty trailers to be used as a variety of interiors. If you're lucky, you'll find an old model for under $10,000. The 2001 models, made by Airstream, a division of Thor Industries, are aluminum-bodied trailers that run about $45,000 for a 16-foot (4.9-meter) single-axle model.

There's a huge network of support for vintage Airstream owners, so if you're thinking about introducing one into your workspace, purchasing and restoration help is a phone call or mouse click away. You'll need to know the tips on restoring a vintage Airstream trailer, whether you take it on the road for a true mobile office, or install it inside a building to resemble Gould Evans's Phoenix office conference room. For example, to remove a dent from a vintage Airstream is not easy, nor is it inexpensive—panels need to be removed by drilling out old rivets, and replacement parts may be hard to find.

Airstreams, when delivered from the factory many years ago, had the natural polished finish of the aircraft aluminum sheets. The shining surface of the trailer in the Gould Evans office reflects lights from the ceiling.

"Devoting full attention to a problem is not the best recipe for having creative thoughts." Mihaly Csikszentmihalyi, author, Creativity

WORKS OF A BON VIVANT
WORK/LIVE LOFT

Parisians are used to elegant, sumptuous apartments and workspaces. Loft living, French-style, has become an alternative that this homeowner and creative artist wanted to live and work in. The owner, therefore, sought an abandoned factory, found one in the outskirts of Paris, and converted the commercial space into a live/work accommodation fit for a serious sensualist.

This former factory has been gutted and redesigned complete with its own swimming pool for exercise, but also for photography settings and meetings. Although there are neither doors nor partitions, the space is divided into four areas including the bedroom with its double shower, which is separated from the living and dining area by a fireplace and low wall. A bar, which conceals a double sink, divides the galley kitchen from the living area. The fully equipped gym, with sauna and Jacuzzi, shares a large alcove with an adjoining small bedroom and opens onto the swimming pool.

Angled corners at each end soften the pool's shape. Two large lamps next to a fireplace at the end of the pool create a warm spot to dry off. Mirror-glass placed at the end of the loft doubles the light reflection and size of the space. The glass roof is the only source of natural light in the loft—nothing interrupts the line of the walls, with the exception of a large, opaque glass entrance door. On sunny days, the roof can be rolled back, allowing the swimming pool area to be open to the sky. The swimming pool measures 29.5 feet (9 meters) in length, 9.8 feet (3 meters) in width and 4.95 feet (1.5 meters) in depth.

"I don't know anybody who doesn't have a fantasy. Everybody must have a fantasy."
Andy Warhol, artist, author, filmmaker

There's an abundance of shelving (80 centimeters or 31.5 inches) that runs the length of the walls throughout the office and living space. This simple idea eliminates the need for much freestanding furniture that clutters a room, such as desks, kitchen units, and bookshelves.

CREATING A POOL HALL

Large, durable, and easy to clean, white ceramic tiles on the floor and walls dominate the space, punctuated by the black leather sofas and touches of yellow color everywhere. The glass furnishings enhance the feeling of space and light.

Steam generated from the pool heating system recycled into a hot air system warms the whole loft. A fireplace at each end of the loft, in which a gas-powered flame burns on heat-resistant stones, gives off more warmth.

There is also a long shelving unit where books and papers can be spread out more easily. In the kitchen the same principle has been adopted for the workstation where preserves, crockery, and utensils can be hidden away. Bar stools allow breakfast to be taken informally, and the fixture is a marine lamp.

SPECS
PRESSURE COOKER

It's not uncommon to spot a business meeting in a pool or sauna in Europe. In fact, saunas play such an important a role in Finland that many business decisions and ideas are made there. New for one Finnish company is the idea of installing a Web camera for videoconferencing into a sauna. Media Tampere, a digital media development group in Helskinki, is outfitting a sauna for four bathers with a portable Web camera and microphone. To follow the development and building of this unique sauna log on to **www.mediaompere.fi/** and click on InternetSauna. Though Finns traditionally enjoy the sauna experience "au natural," these sauna-goers may prefer to wear their business suits to these steamy meetings.

The kitchen doubles as a café for visiting clients. Open shelving eliminates the need for cabinets, but also invites business guests to feel more at home by helping themselves to refreshments during meetings.

"I offer images; I conjure memories of freedom that can still be reached."

Jim Morrison, musician

FIGMENTS OF THE IMAGINATION
CTV

Watching television is already enough fantasy for most of us. But, working on premises for a broadcast company is quite another thing. You are creating an experience of fantasy for others to enjoy, so the work environment should be anything but sterile and staid. In fact, the space should celebrate and encourage fun and fantasy.

That's the idea behind CTV's Agincourt, Ontario, studio. CTV Inc. is one of three main television networks in Canada, a division of Bell Globemedia, a multimedia company integrating TV, Internet, and print products. "I wanted to create a nice, fresh, open space to allow for creativity and communication between all employees," Susan Mason, director of building facilities, says.

Marshall Cummings took on the 200,000-square-foot (18,580-square-meter) space. Since each individual programming department had its own work processes, Mason's idea was to create a linking neighborhood environment and community where all the departments would feel like they were part of one cause, one team, and allow them to intermingle throughout the day.

"One of the most interesting phenomena is one of the wider hallways we designed," Mason says. "There's an 8-foot-wide [2.4-meter-wide] hallway where there's almost always twenty or so people standing around in different groups just talking with one another." If she ever had the opportunity to build out another wide hallway, Mason says she would do it since it's one of the easiest, least intrusive ways to encourage spontaneous communication between people.

A creative workspace doesn't have to be expensive or intricate. The Canadian Discovery Channel, part of CTV, asked to have installed floor-to-ceiling graphics of wildlife, underwater, and space scenes as a way to creatively jazz up the open space. It proved quite a dramatic display. "They put their own mark on the space, and it's inspiring to them, and that's what counts," Mason says.

Employees at CTV mingle with one another, and with broadcast celebrities at the same time. Life-like cutouts of stars, such as *The Sopranos* lead, James Gandolfini, dot the hallways. The cutouts weren't part of the original design, but U.S. distributors gave them to the programming department, and they were immediately integrated into the workspace.

CTV is a twenty-four-hour operation. There's a mix of studio space, workspace, and support areas. Everyone is encouraged to mingle at all hours, even at the foos-ball table, for the possible cross-pollination of ideas. It's often reported that the area can become quite boisterous at times, Susan Mason says. That's how she knows it's a popular spot.

"We become what we behold. We shape our tools and then our tools shape us."
Marshall McLuhan, author

You never know whom you'll bump into at CTV's headquarters.
Actor Harrison Ford makes a surprise appearance in the hallway
in the form of a life-size cutout.

> "The theater is so endlessly fascinating because it's so accidental. It's so much like life."
>
> Arthur Miller, playwright

EXPERIMENTAL THEATER
YOUNG & RUBICAM, FORD, AND HAWORTH COLLABORATION

Imagine trying to conduct long team meetings in a space that measures only 8 feet by 9 feet (2.4 meters by 2.7 meters). It would be tough to cram a group of people in that small space to spend hours brainstorming creative solutions for a client. But that's just what the Young & Rubicam/Ford teams faced in their old offices.

SPACE SHORTAGE PROBLEMS

The lack of space was palpable. Meeting rooms were in extremely short supply, and oftentimes, teams were left to meet in a break room or isolated section of a hallway. Each team had an assigned 72-square-foot (6.68-square-meter) walled space to be used as a work area, and individual workspaces measured about 16 square feet (1.5 square meter). Employees described the atmosphere as "tense," because the working conditions were so unpleasant. When Ford wanted to divide and overhaul its Lincoln and Mercury brands, the agency decided to relocate the firm from Detroit to Los Angeles for a fresh perspective.

Haworth worked with its in-house Ideation group (a group of cognitive ergonomists, social psychologists, and designers) and the Idea Factory to design and create two identical spaces to serve as the theater for each brand—one room for the Lincoln team, the other for Mercury. Each brand, with approximately five teams working on various projects at any given time, was able to use the rooms.

UNCLUTTERING THE MIND

The spaces are organized and designed to help make the "mind" of the brand visible to each team member and client. Each room also provides a dynamic theater for presenting new concepts to Ford executives because the client becomes immersed in the environment in which the brainstorming takes place.

Carving space out of the air for these two teams brings them together in more ways than anyone could have imagined. Friday afternoons, the theater of the brand turns off the stage lights, closes the curtains, and builds team camaraderie by throwing themselves a cast party.

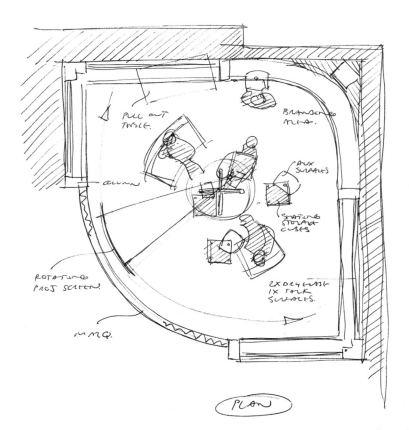

Curtains visually isolate each team room from non-team members, which minimized the number of undesired interruptions. Team members have described these settings as a "theater of the brand," and a stage "where the brand lives and breathes."

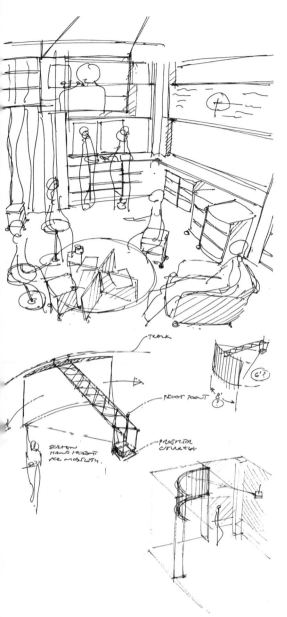

A round table with a frosted glass top is the gathering spot in each room. The way the rooms are set up encourages increased eye contact, leading to freer flow of conversation and ideas. For additional comfort, each room has a lounge chair and a couch as well as six height-adjustable stools and four cubes that can be used for seating and storage areas.

Teams say they feel the display areas in each room make it easier to read and analyze data for trends, patterns, and comparisons. The most popular aspects of the team rooms are the white boards, tack boards, and the movable furniture. Each white board and tack board is 3 feet by 10 feet (.9 meters by 3 meters). A long, curved tack board can be raised and lowered. Behind this board is another tack board with shelves for artifacts.

GOALS FOR REDESIGN

WISH LIST FOR TEAM ROOMS:

- Room for a variety of tasks—from brainstorming sessions to planning media campaigns to group meetings and presentations to clients. Solution—each room is 625 square feet (58 meters).
- Way to visually isolate team rooms. Solution—curtains.
- Ability to leave works-in-progress in team rooms between meetings. Solution—rolling white boards provide layers of storage.
- Way for team members to feel comfortable enough to participate freely and openly in each gathering. Solution—round table, lounge chairs.

RESULTS OF REDESIGN

- The design of the rooms promotes eye contact among team members.
- The rate of participation in meetings seems higher.
- Team members feel "special" for the sheer fact that team rooms are available.
- Several team members interviewed by Haworth in the post-occupancy report said their most successful collaborative and creative experiences have been in the team rooms.
- Team members feel that the rooms indicate to clients that the agency is innovative because it easily illustrates how the brand teams work and think together.
- The consensus among interviewees was that the work done in the team rooms is of a higher quality than similar work done in other environments.

"The gift of fantasy has meant more to me than my talent for absorbing positive knowledge." Albert Einstein, physicist

THE STARSHIP ENTERPRISE
DUFFY DESIGN

A branch of the Minneapolis-based graphics design firm and part of Fallon New York, an advertising agency, Duffy Design found space in The Woolworth Building, a New York City landmark skyscraper. Duffy retained MAP, a young design firm, to create an interior that exuded the company's image of cutting-edge design. The fluid lines and circular design of the space is as fresh and modern as Duffy's clean, modern graphic design. Since Duffy specializes in creating brand identities, it wanted to be an active collaborator with MAP in developing its own image. The space-age imagery gives visitors and employees the perception that they've entered a trend-conscious world above the rest.

WELCOME TO THE OUTER LIMITS

Once off the elevator, employees and visitors are lost in space, as they leave the noisy world of Manhattan behind and enter another universe floating above the earthly urban streets. The interior is filled with organic-shaped elements. Although MAP prepared the entire 20,000-square-foot (1,858-square-meter) floor for occupancy, this area called for the fit-out of only one-third of the space for Duffy's thirty-person staff. The design theme is announced in the circular reception area and desk with its suggestion of a command center, and it continues in the central gallery corridor with curved walls gently enveloping anyone walking through.

At the end of the gallery passageway is the main work area, which consists of three groups of eight open workstations connected by floor-to-ceiling portals that allow communication by sight and sound along its entire length. Duffy prides itself on its team approach to design campaigns, and MAP designed this high-tech, open environment to support that work philosophy.

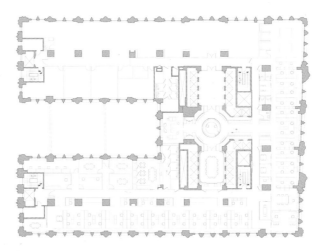

In this floor plan, an open work area is joined by a library, private office, and game room along the front window wall. A series of small conference rooms and private telephone rooms, with floor-to-ceiling windows and glass doors, let natural light shine through and reach the center of the floor.

A circular desk in the reception area, highlighted by a round drop ceiling overhead, is the command center for the office. Four areas, including the elevator, spin off from the organically shaped desk area. A casual seating room, a conference room, and a passageway leads directly into the offices. Monitors in the passageway display the company's designs.

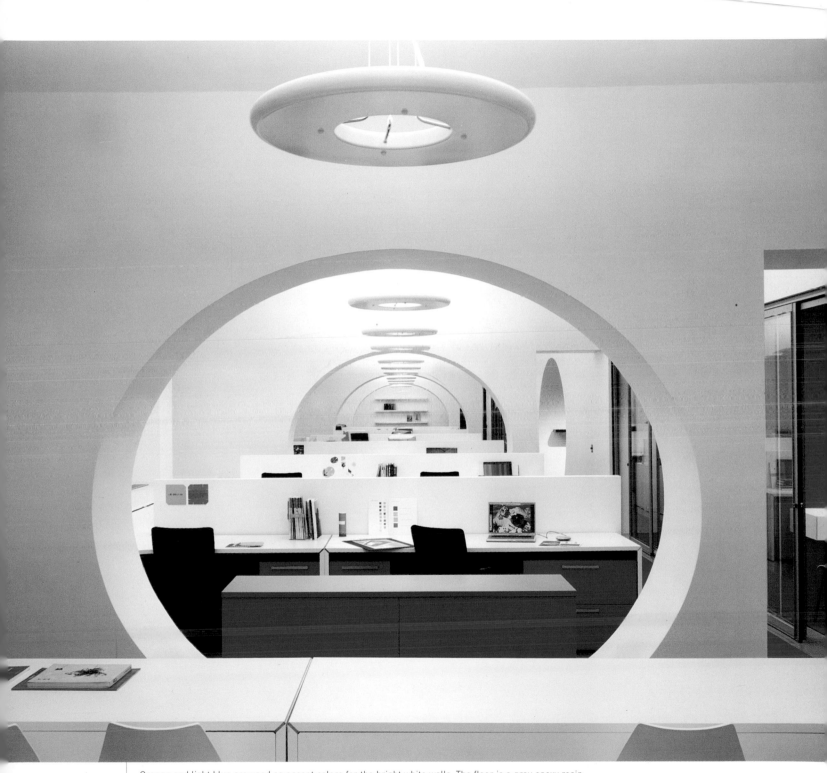

Orange and light blue are used as accent colors for the bright white walls. The floor is a gray epoxy resin and the simple custom desks and tables are topped with white laminate. Orange cabinetry and carpeting is used judiciously throughout the space as a way to bring in excitement in an otherwise cool-colored interior. The orange is bright, and compliments the powder blue flat painted walls. To the right of the workstations is a bank of small, private phone booths with sliding glass doors.

There are large conference rooms directly off the reception area and staff meeting areas and a kitchen and dining room extending down one side of the U-shaped floor. The largest of the conference rooms is the presentation room, equipped with a rear projection screen, surround sound, remote control lighting, and magnetic white board wall panels. The table, custom designed by MAP for the space, repeats the curved corners of the room.

> ## "The most important thing about Spaceship Earth—an instruction book didn't come with it."
> R. Buckminster Fuller, architect and inventor of the geodesic dome

Squares of color behind the reception desk are colored lights to simulate a modern version of stained glass. The entire Fallon workspace is washed over with light to create an ethereal environment, a place to incubate fresh and bright ideas.

HEAVEN-SENT

Downstairs from Duffy, the offices of its parent company, Fallon New York, have a celestial and surreal feel to the workspace, designed by MAP, as well. A major advertising agency, Fallon moved into the Woolworth Building to accommodate its growth and to be near Duffy. The agency's interiors express its identity with the theme of light and openness as metaphors for the creation of ideas. Morris Adjmi of MAP says he and his design team interpreted those images in a luminous environment that floats with open office spaces and light-infused areas throughout the 28,000-square-foot (2,601-square-meter) workplace. Though it doesn't have the space age imagery of Duffy, the Fallon office space in its own way lifts the visitor out of the urban world and into a light-saturated planet high above the streets of New York City.

The space is distinguished by specialty lighting. Two 15-foot-long (4.6-meter-long) illuminated rosewood and glass tables in the reception area highlight graphics and products. Walls of acrylic and wood in the elevator lobby and fabric walls in the open work areas are illuminated in blocks of red, green, yellow, and blue light. The hallway leading to the main presentation rooms has staggered light panels with display advertising graphics.

> "Creativity requires the courage to let go of certainties."
> Erich Fromm, psychoanalyst

Gels of intense red, pink, and orange wash over an otherwise blank white wall. At the end of the hallway, a conference room has a translucent glass cabinet that acts as a wall and holds a flat-screen monitor that seems suspended in air.

AN INTENSE EXPERIENCE
HERMAN MILLER CHICAGO SHOWROOM

The workplace. The office. We've seen volumes of information about those subjects in the past decade. Like with any overcrowded market, how do you make your message stand out, especially when it's an important one? That's what Herman Miller had to contend with when redesigning its Chicago showroom for Neocon (the major annual trade show for commercial architects, designers, and facility professionals). Herman Miller had a message about workplace innovation, and it needed to shout it out in a 25,000-square-foot (2,323-square-meter) space in the Merchandise Mart. Why not put on a show? thought Mark Sexton, of the design firm Krueck & Sexton. The result was a theatrical production using a kaleidoscope of colors to grab the attention of busy show goers.

COLOR THE WORK WORLD

Herman Miller was eager to introduce Resolve, a workstation designed around the creative needs and wants of workers. Resolve, designed by Ayse Birsel, principal of the New York City design firm Olive 1:1, is a simple system that gives people creative and easy-to-achieve design possibilities including many levels of enclosure or openness, depending on the user's needs. And the furniture manufacturer used dramatic color to invite clients in to experience the welcoming nature of Resolve.

To grab attention, even the corridor lights outside the Herman Miller showroom were dimmed considerably to let the electric colors take center stage and shine through the glass windows. Once inside, colored lights flooded the space. As visitors walked toward the back of the showroom, the color lights softened and focused on the products on display.

To make the light show a success, the showroom, without lighting, was a white-painted box with neutral colored flooring. A minimal amount of detailing was used throughout the space, except for the table of flowers with a fragrance that helped heighten, yet relax, the experience at the same time.

"With color, one obtains an energy that seems to stem from witchcraft."
Henri Matisse, artist and author

"Ideas move rapidly when their time comes." Carolyn Heilbrun, feminist scholar

Resolve's canopies and screens were digitally printed and colored using the colors of the lighting in the showroom lobby. The capability of customizing the image on workspace dividing screens opens up entirely new dimensions in workplace design. Porch lights on poles tell people if someone is "home" or not.

The immersion wall projects images of products, meant to engage the viewer in concepts and ideas. The only accessory in the lobby—a table of fragrant roses—is the same color as hues projected on the walls.

Visitors who need a soothing respite from the color infusion out front relax in the peaceful white lounge. The only color in the room is in the large upholstered chairs.

INSPIRED DESIGN: RETHINKING THE CUBICLE

Herman Miller and designer Ayse Birsel saw the sweeping and ongoing changes in how people work, the rise in collaborative work, and the expansion at such a fast pace of complex technology. Taken together, it was a timely opportunity to reexamine how the work environment works, or doesn't work at all.

The team knew they couldn't come up with yet another panel-based system. Instead, they created an anti-panel system. Resolve is based on poles with screens attached at generous 120-degree angles (think of the shape of honeycombs and snowflakes to get the idea), unlike the tighter, more severe ninety-degree angle of most cubicle walls. This approach helps users move screens based on work style needs. At the same time, the design uses far less material and space than traditional panel systems. Gone are the traditional right-angled, paneled cubicles; instead, each Resolve constellation is shaped how the worker wants it to be shaped.

Workstations are designed to be lowered or raised to sitting or standing positions. Like the modern Volkswagen Bug and famed trend-spotter Faith Popcorn's home office furniture collection for Hooker Furniture, Resolve also features little details that count,

such as small bud vases that attach to ea[ch...] "porch lights" for groups of colleagues. T[...] to create both a greater sense of commun[...]

The screens are the stars of the Resolve line. Translucent boundary, rolling flags, and canopy screens offer enclosure without cutting off natural light. Resolve does away with the typical corporate panel fabric used extensively in panel systems. Instead, screens may be digitally printed to display a number of graphic treatments. The existing collection of designs includes images prepared by Jhane Barnes, Eric Ludlum, Joyce Mast, and the Digital Atelier, as well as a select group from Herman Miller designers. The collections feature images that are graphic, abstract, or photographic, and can be mixed and matched for unusual effects. Clients are free to design their own ideas, product branding, slogans, and colors, as well.

The success of Resolve has landed the collection in the permanent collection of New York City's Museum of Modern Art collection, along with the company's ubiquitous Aeron ergonomic chair, and helped to earn Birsel the Brooklyn Museum of Art Young Designer Award for 2001.

Resolve's rolling screens offer privacy and enclosure at the same time. Screens displace walls and create immediate space where necessary. Here, colored lighting gives the screens a pink and orange undertone. Boomerang work surfaces ensure that work tools and papers are easily within reach of the user, yet don't create a claustrophobic feeling, either.

NURTURING COLORS

The Color Marketing Group (CMG) in Alexandria, Virginia, maintains that employees who work on computers all day long prefer softer, lighter colors that are nurturing and remind them of home. CMG predicts that pinks — tones that are neutral or a sophisticated, such as warmer silver-pink — will become more popular in the office. The research firm says that colors that remind employees of the calming influence of water, such as aqueous greens and iridescent blues, will also become more common in the workplace.

CMG's research offers more direction on using color as a nurturing element in the workplace:

- Orange is a welcoming color and connotes informality and playfulness. It's best used in a common conversation area.
- Pink acts as a tranquilizer and is a soothing color for high-stress environments such as call centers.
- Yellow is happy and energetic.
- Blues lower blood pressure and pulse rates, and are considered relaxing colors, best used in relaxation areas rather than in high-energy workspaces.
- Green is refreshing and works anywhere.

DREAM HOUSE
EVANS GROUP HEADQUARTERS

Designing a dream house is one thing, but creating an entire dream village inside a building is quite another. But that's what the design firm the Evans Group did for its associates who own for the workday a piece of the American dream, even if it's in the workplace.

This 16,000-square-foot (1,486-square-meter) structure located in downtown Orlando was envisioned at first to be a "biosphere" working environment where the occupants would have clean air, sunny conditions, and a green place in which to work. The building was then designed and specified to make sure it was built in a healthy manner with energy conscious components, as well. As it evolved, the building grew as an environment to make one feel as if they were walking down an old village-style street, encountering homes along the way.

The conference room is engulfed by live foliage and windows to make workers feel like they are meeting in a backyard greenhouse.

Inside the building is a village of employee houses. Each house-office
looks like a traditional house, complete with siding, shutters, and gardens.
There are no roofs on the house-offices to keep the air circulating.

The main boulevard terminates at the town library and theater, which is the firm's boardroom, with video conferencing, surround sound, DVD, and VCR.

Below, a ficus tree grows out of the wood reception desk.

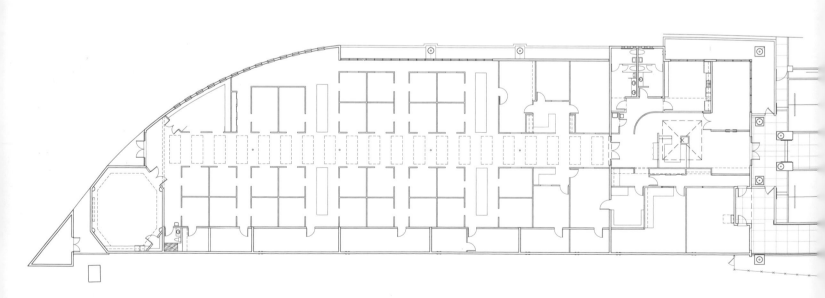

The main circulation of the village is the Boulevard of Dreams, a cobblestone street complete with streetlights, park benches, full-grown ficus trees, street signs, and architectural facades.

FANTASY TOWNSHIP

The layout begins with the public spaces, such as the reception area, garden conference room, kitchen, and break room. The reception area is complete with a full-grown ficus tree growing out of the custom, maple reception desk towards the large pyramid skylight overhead.

What's striking about the space is the work "village," as the design firm calls it. Visitors pass through a glass wall in the reception area into the village. Each employee has a house complete with doors, windows, shutters, roof tile, and a flower box—all the makings of home. Even the restrooms are atypical, treated like gardens with murals depicting lush greenery and marine life.

The site is in the middle of one of the busiest intersections in downtown, next to a noisy railroad track, but the sound does not interfere with the workplace thanks to the thoughtful floor plan. The major window walls of the building face north toward a downtown park, allowing spectacular views, while the south side of the building is a solid, windowless wall running parallel along the heavily used train tracks. To further insulate against the noise, the building was designed with a 10-foot (3-meter) barrier of storage rooms running its entire south side.

The building's main material is concrete block, filled with vermiculite, and an exposed bar joist roof system, tile floors, and glass curtain walls.

THE SERENE WORKSPACE

WHERE PEOPLE FIND CALM SANCTUARY AND PEACE

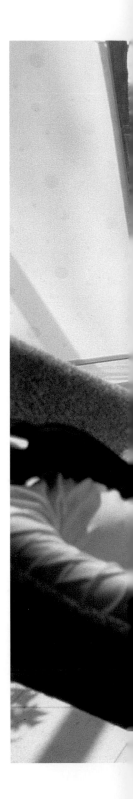

A serene workspace is designed to calm the mind of the worker. It takes the employee away from the noise and distraction of office life and creates an oasis to which the mind can go to quiet down until the choppy waters of the brain are calm enough to let a sense of creativity emerge. It's a sanctuary to renew and rejuvenate spirit, allowing employees to untangle the tight knots of work problems and reweave the loosened threads into silky patterns saturated with creative solutions.

In light of our world's changed history, it's no wonder we may feel a sense of hesitance when we step into an elevator to take us to our offices. Suddenly, how large our office is, how chic our furnishings, how shiny our windows, mean little when we think of the alternative. But a little safety, a little serenity in the workplace, can make it easier to be there, to feel a sense of nourishment, of stillness where everything is okay for the moment.

You can audibly hear the sighs of those who find solace in a serene workspace. The worker who needs quiet steps into this carefully crafted place of tranquility and feels safe enough to exhale out the internal toxins and pressures of the problem at hand. Once a worker is in this space, they can now hear the quiet of the small, internal voice, the one that has all the answers to their creative problems.

Serene workspaces help employees reach their spiritual side, the one that helps them trust in their own creativity. Companies that understand the power of spirituality offer employees retreat-like spaces to dwell when necessary, offices inspired by nature, chapels in which to meditate and pray, and outlets, such as walking paths and exercise studios, that promote mind-body integration.

The following serene workspaces are tranquil environments in which creative work is inspired. An artist's retreat in Denmark was designed taking into consideration all that is necessary for artists to create, including the lush and dynamic piece of land on which it was built, and the way the light streams in at all times during the day and night. The Essex Conference Center & Retreat is a sanctuary away from the everyday business world. It was designed specifically to help guests slow down their insistent mind chatter so they can hear inner whisperings and insights necessary for brainstorming. A new media company, HBG New Media, has created an environment that seems to be calmly suspended in space, giving employees room to think and decompress, atypical of many frenetic dot.com office spaces that have gone by the wayside. And a sculptor, Stephen Hendee, turns a conference room into a spiritual center when he designs a space that relaxes the mind while stimulating the creative senses using lighting. From conference center to conference room, each project shown has an element of tranquility to help employees find a sense of peacefulness during the workday.

"It may be that those who do most, dream most." Stephen Leacock, Canadian humorist and educator

DO NOT DISTURB
ARTIST'S RETREAT, VEJBY, DENMARK

Contemporary art dealer Mikael Andersen knows what it takes to produce meaningful art from deep within the soul. For many artists, it takes working and creating in an atmosphere of solitude and serenity. He commissioned Henning Larsens Tegnestue, an international design firm in Copenhagen, to design a retreat nearby in the seaside community of Vejby, far from the noisy, busy urban area of Copenhagen. The goal: To create a pastoral respite in which artists contemplate and conceive their work.

TAKING ADVANTAGE OF LANDSCAPE

The location seemed far from ideal at first. The first time the architect, Peer Jeppesen, visited the area where Andersen wanted to build, it was a cold winter day with harsh northerly winds. It seemed impossible to reach the slope because of the strong winds. But the site was so lovely, 150 feet (46 meters) high above the sea; it was hard to resist the challenge of designing a tranquility zone for artists high above the earth. The property is set back a bit from the coast in a small carved-out hollow with a view toward the northwest over a public lookout area—a perfect spot for outdoor meditation and creative thought.

The 1,000-square-foot (93-square-meters) retreat was designed as one very large space with four sliding doors that subdivides the house into four rooms including a studio, living room, entry, and kitchen. The core of the house contains all the mechanics, including two fireplaces/wood stoves, a bath, and kitchen niche. A bathroom is lit during the day by a skylight. The spaces are furnished with a few elegant, yet lightweight, pieces that can be easily moved around as the artist sees fit.

MOOD LIGHTING

To help artists work inside, the designers created a space where light can be manipulated. The 400-square-foot (37-square meter) artist studio is on the north side. The north end wall has high windows, and a low band of windows in the same wall lets low light stream in, which brightens up the studio's floor. Side lighting comes from the west through two floor-to-ceiling windows. From the studio, kitchen, and living room, there's access to the large west terrace from which the inhabitant can enjoy a sunset. The space is never monotone; each room is always cast in a different light during different times of the day.

> "By listening to the creator within, we are led to our right path."
> Julia Cameron, author, *The Artist's Way*

The timber-frame house with steel bracing sits high on a bluff. Exterior siding is local larch wood, which will patina over time into a fine, silver-gray color that will harmonize with the undergrowth of blue cornflowers and 200 birch trees planted on the property. Large terraces, such as this one on the south wall, are built over thick fern growth.

"The primary distinction of the artist is that he must actively cultivate that state which most men, necessarily, must avoid: the state of being alone."

James Baldwin, author, playwright and civil rights activist

The interior walls and ceilings are covered in birch plywood. The studio in the north end of the house is designed so that one wall is almost completely closed to create a feeling of privacy, yet lets natural light in through low-placed windows to illuminate only the floor space on which the artist is working.

A wooden, tilting awning with slats covers the west-facing terrace. The house has many sliding, rotating, and movable surfaces that let the artist manipulate interior and exterior light and privacy.

"All truly great thoughts are conceived by walking."
Friedrich Wilhelm Nietzsche, German philosopher

The size of a room can make or break a team meeting, says Gersh, who has an extensive background in education. This small room is ideal for intimate meetings where the goal is to contain the energy of the group. Putting small groups in larger rooms tends to make everyone feel unfocused, and the energy is scattered and diluted.

OPEN-AIR POLICY
THE ESSEX CONFERENCE CENTER & RETREAT

Stephen Gersh, truly considered by all who know him to be a Renaissance man, began building the eighteen-acre Essex Conference Center & Retreat thirty-five years ago. He built every square inch of the two main buildings, including the spa and sauna, using cedar and hemlock that were found on the grounds then milled into beams. His wife, Judith Arisman, a graphic designer, continues to take care of the interiors, from the wall coverings and carpeting, down to the tablecloths and bedspreads. Natural light and nature's materials, including the room built around bits of boulders that protrude through the floor and walls, reign in every nook and cranny of the conference center. Together, Gersh and Arisman run one of the most successful conference centers catering mostly to Boston business people who need to be rescued from the city and taken into the deep woods where they can be re-energized. At the center, new ideas are fostered, the spirit revitalized, and personal and organizational growth encouraged.

"The natural light, fresh air, soft hues are all meant to create a sense of calmness and relaxation to help guests move inward towards their creativity."

Stephen Gersh, director of the Essex Conference Center & Retreat

SHEDDING CORPORATE TRAPPINGS

A workspace this serene—designed to soothe the corporate soul—did not happen by accident. The compound's history is colorful, often housing artists and other socially responsible groups that needed meeting places. The center found its way to corporate America by word of mouth, and Gersh and Arisman are quick to tell potential clients that the experience is quite *unlike* that of a hotel with conferencing facilities. For one, the center has a capacity for thirty-eight people, and Gersh has no intention of increasing the space because he doesn't want to compromise on the quality and energy of the staff in order to serve "throngs of people."

The guests' experience starts when they turn into the skinny, dirt driveway of the center. The curvaceous road is intentional, Gersh says, meant to slow guests down.

Parking is located away from accommodations so guests have a chance to leave their car behind and enjoy the surrounding landscape. The ocean is to the left and behind a forest of lush trees that have carved into the grounds are "pods" of space for small meetings or deep meditation. The ropes course is across the grounds for guests who are there to build trust among colleagues. A campfire with tree stumps for seating sits near the building with the spa and sauna.

There's an abundance of oversized windows to help guests drink in the natural surroundings even when inside during meetings. Bedrooms are simple, bordering on sparse. Dispensing with the fancy room amenities and oversized closets is also intentional. It helps guests leave behind their mainstream world of luxury so they can find their inner world of simplicity and creativity.

> "Slow down, think clearly, learn more."
> Stephen Gersh, director of the Essex Conference Center & Retreat

STUDYING BEHAVIORS

Over the years, Gersh observed rituals. He notes that male guests come into the center and immediately remove their ties, change into casual wear, and sit down to talk with one another. "Competitiveness drops here," he says. Female guests, on the other hand, want to be more formal when they come to the center. However, he notes that female guests are more adaptable to their environment. Now, Gersh's team sends out packages with suggestions on what type of clothing to bring.

Gersh's guests tend to absorb that relaxed feeling immediately, he says. "People tend to sit around at the dinner tables for two to three hours, talking, having fun."

Gersh has noticed a positive change in the corporate groups he encounters at the center. "They are less uptight than they were ten years ago," he says, and attributes that to the great strides that corporate America has made in its quests for innovation and creativity over the past two decades. "That has an overall effect on society and on its employees," he says.

Stephen Gersh, the center's director, built the post and beam center with his own hands, using over 4,000 timbers of standing dead cedar and hemlock, which was found on the property and milled. Guests tend to move flip charts outside in the fall and spring or go find spots in the deep woods for brainstorming meetings.

SPECS
AT THE CENTER OF **SERENITY**

There are two basic tenets that have guided Gersh and Arisman in the creation of an environment where guests who are there for strategy planning and team building can experience breakthroughs and insights.

1. HEALTHY NOURISHMENT

Gersh and Arisman say food is more than just something to give guests energy. "We cook from the heart," Gersh says. "We believe that food nurtures, warms, supports you, and brings back memories." The food that the conference center serves is always whole and organic, and no beef is allowed on the premises. There's not even a deep fryer in the kitchen. "We are getting more and more vegetarian requests," Gersh says. Evening meals are served on tables with white tablecloths and glowing candles, a small ritual meant to give guests a special dining experience. After hours, the conference center has set up a casual campfire area with tree trunks that double as chairs. Guests are encouraged to eat S'mores and marshmallows around the fire while telling stories as a way of bonding.

2. SIMPLE DECOR

Though the ordinary office is often sterile, full of cubicles and unwanted distractions, Gersh says the center's interiors are meant to be anything but boring. It's rare to find a manmade material or surface in the wood structures. In addition, the facility is designed and operated in an environmentally responsible manner that includes using toxic-free cleaning products; energy-saving compact fluorescent bulbs in most of the fixtures; a sauna that is heated with non-treated wood scraps from construction projects, standing dead wood, and limbs; among other recycling programs. "There's touchability here, people love to touch the wood surfaces, they feel safe and secure in a structure that is all natural," says Gersh of the habitat. Gersh even built certain rooms around the huge boulders that wouldn't budge out of the way, so the stone becomes part of the interior decor. The inside of the main building and spa is really an extension of the outdoors. And, from inside, at all different vantages, guests can see the Japanese pond, smell the garden and the ocean water, and hear the waterfall just minutes away from the main building.

The center "unteaches and uneducates" guests to rid them of images from mainstream life so they can uncover their own uniqueness and express their inherent creativity and trusting. The goal of the center's design is to get guests to have fun. "Why suffer to learn and change?" asks Gersh, "Having fun means having an enjoyable, thrilling, exciting experience in finding out something different and new about your job or a colleague."

DEEP COUNTRY, DEEP THOUGHT
THE CONFERENCE BARN

Architect Michael Sant, Sant Architects, was asked to create a tranquil work area for the client, a corporate executive and chairman of his family foundation, and his wife, president of the foundation. Luckily, the clients were Sant's own father and stepmother, and he knew of their needs for solace and serenity in their workspace, plus their commitment to environmentalism and nature's surroundings. Sant had the advantage over the original architect hired for the project of understanding the clients' need for a domestic building with the rugged qualities required of a brainstorming barn.

A PLACE TO CONTEMPLATE

The small, intimate space would become a meeting space set somewhere in the 117 acres of a nineteenth-century Virginia horse farm to comfortably accommodate as many as sixteen people at a time. The space, to be known as the "conference barn," is a structure of striking simplicity and poignancy. The barn houses the family foundation, which focuses on solving and dealing with environmental issues, and also became a place for relaxed thought and contemplation. So much so, that Sant says his clients rarely leave the space to go back to the nearby farmhouse. Along with the barn and farmhouse on the property is a guest cottage and stucco stable in a similar style.

A decision was made to place the new building southeast of the main stable and relate the two buildings formally. A series of reclaimed Douglas fir columns and trusses, set upon a radiantly heated bluestone plinth, defines the building's structure, while a ribbon of fir sliding doors surrounds the structure's occupants with nature. To modulate sun and privacy, slatted wood shutters, balanced by cast-iron counterweights, slide vertically on the centers of the columns.

The services for the building are concealed within two refined plywood cabinets, giving the structure its tripartite configuration. A kitchenette, water closet, audio-visual cabinet, and mechanical ducting are housed within these monolithic slabs. The boilers and air-handling units are located in the main stable. The water for the radiant slab is preheated by a solar system in the nearby paddock.

The beauty of this design is that the sliding glass doors and a shutter system allow the clients to open the pavilion to nature's surroundings, indeed an inspiration for creative thinking.

A wood-strip canoe, wrapped in translucent fabric with fluorescent tubes inside and suspended below a continuous ridge skylight, echoes the simplicity of the structure and provides a soft, sculptural, light source for the barn's interior

"To accomplish great things we must not only act, but also dream. Not only plan, but also believe."
Anatole France, French writer

The 7.5-foot-high (2.28-meter-high) doors of glass diminish the boundary between outdoors and indoors. The plywood storage cabinet with Douglas fir veneer acts as a divider between the conferencing area with its upholstered furnishings, and the workspace.

The 20-foot by 50-foot (6-meter by 15-meter) pavilion is a box-like, glass house topped by a gabled roof of terne-coated, stainless steel with a full-length skylight. The barn is situated on a floor of local bluestone. The foundation is stacked fieldstone gathered from the surrounding property.

CATHEDRAL OF CREATIVITY
MEDITATION/CONFERENCE ROOM

Everything Stephen Zades thought he knew about architecture and space changed the day he stepped foot into an art exhibit at PS1 in New York City. Zades, the former CEO of Long Haymes Carr Advertising (before it merged with Mullen in 2001), and founder of the Odyssey Group, a creative consulting firm, was frazzled from his ride on the subway, and not impressed as he trudged into PS1, a big, cold warehouse of a space popular to art exhibits. But inside to view the exhibit at the time, he had a strange sensation when he walked into a large, glowing geometric cavern sculpture by Stephen Hendee, an artist from Newark, New Jersey. "I felt like I had stepped into the safety of a womb, yet I felt invigorated at the same time," remembers Zades; he lingered inside the oversized sculpture.

It was an experiment with space, and every element of the sculpture was stimulating, yet soothing at the same time, Zades says, and that is one difficult objective to achieve with design. Hendee, a sculptor, began fabricating small geometric shapes until they grew in size so that people could actually walk inside the work. His large-scale sculptures are like warmly lit igloos — an effect achieved by diffusing light through foam board and creating a casual geometric motif with adhesive tape. Though Hendee never created a usable room from his sculptures before, he agreed to take the commission to create a conference space based on his art.

TAKING A RISK

What Zades had in mind was a conference room in the ad agency where people could feel relaxed, yet stimulated enough to dream and brainstorm at the same time. Hendee's hypnotic sculptures were just the answer. Hendee didn't think much of traditional conference rooms at the time. "Conference rooms are about as nice as football locker rooms," he says. Some people in the agency were skeptical of Hendee's work. They weren't sure if big ideas could be found in a windowless room of foam and electrical tape. Even Hendee was skeptical that anyone would accept a conference room as art. "It's a cheap, inventive way to realize an unusual, creative space," Hendee says. "Many managers don't want to spend money on something like this, though it costs in total about $10,000, much less than some architecture projects."

SPONTANEOUS WORK OF ART

Hendee created the room not so much by plan, but by spontaneity. The only problem was working around an electrostatic filter in the ceiling. Hendee fit a cowling over it. One of the walls was left bare for hanging documents and sketches during meetings. The result was otherworldly. "The moment you enter the space, it produces a state of change of both mind and body, exactly the frame of mind needed for brainstorming, ideation, and creative problem solving," Zades says.

Hendee designs his walk-in works to be like caverns and cathedrals, meant to create a transcendent, meditative state. But he says you don't have to build a whole room to achieve that nirvana. He makes wall pieces and hanging lights that don't take over a room, but gives someone a point in a room on which to focus and relax.

It's one huge step for creative mankind when the corporate world accepts art into it in the form of an imaginary, translucent universe-cum-conference room. "So many spaces we work and live in have become lifeless and boring," Zades says. "This is one of the many contributions and lessons contemporary art and design brings to the business world."

"It's a space to dream in, to listen in, to imagine in, and to explore in."
Stephen Zades, former CEO, Long Haymes Carr Advertising Agency

Artist Stephen Hendee transformed this unusual, windowless room into a brainstorming chamber by creating a stained-glass–like sculpture out of pieces of back-lit foam board fused with black tape. The structure is delicate—if someone walks into the wall, it may cause a crease that can be fixed by taping it. It took four twelve-hour days for Hendee and an assistant to sculpt the 25-foot by 11-foot (7.5-meter by 3.3-meter) room. The room, which is softly lit by placing saturated gels over fluorescent lights placed behind the foam board, feels safe, not claustrophobic, in part because of the 7-foot-high (2.1-meter-high) ceiling. Hendee says the flickering of fluorescent lights overhead can make people feel drowsy, but, because the walls are lit up, it has the reverse effect on inhabitants and makes them feel awake. A drop of drowsiness relaxes the mind, while the brightness of the room keeps people awake and aware.

A SPIRITUAL PAUSE
TRIPLE 5 SOUL

Walk into Triple 5 Soul, an urban sportswear company that serves fashion-forward artists such as deejays, emcees, and fashion designers, and you'd expect to see a workspace filled with a noisy mix of clamorous colors and vigorous textures. Instead, the space is a clean, clear environment that exudes all the peace and serenity of a retreat center.

UNDERSTATED ELEGANCE

The atmosphere is intentionally understated in order to encourage clarity of soul and creativity of mind, says founder Camella Ehlke. Architect Qui Ly of Iota Office created a vital, yet quietly professional space filled with translucent floating walls and stone floors. The serene location outside of Manhattan helps workers escape the gritty, frenetic, and competitive energy of the Seventh Avenue garment district to help them work at a more inviting pace. And, it's only a ten-minute cab ride to midtown Manhattan.

"Do not follow where the path leads; rather go where there is no path, and leave a trail." David Perkins, author, *The Mind's Best Work*

Soft lighting and a neutral palette create a comfortable open workspace for design and marketing associates. A 200-foot-long (61-meter-long) wall of closets keeps reference materials and rolling racks of samples out of the way behind the scenes.

A clean, white doorway outlined in metal leads into a simple reception area that doubles as a setting for quiet contemplation. A window wall is a grid of glass and acrylic materials that let in soft, diffused daylight onto the rugged stone floor. The custom coffee table keeps order to the area because it has wells to hold magazines so they don't get strewn about.

Clothing is often tucked behind closed doors so that the space remains neat and without clutter. The conference room has a set of floating doors that swing away to expose a large sample area.

"Create your own visual style....Let it be unique for yourself and yet identifiable for others." Orson Welles, actor, director

The sandblasted glass entryway with HBG New Media's logo gives the reception area a solid, elegant, and yet ethereal feel upon entering the office. The client directed the designer to avoid all traditional corporate icons while giving the space an established look.

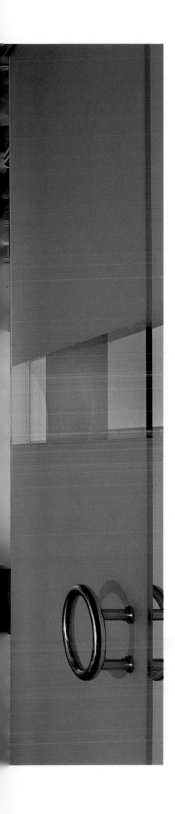

JOURNEY INTO SPACE
HBG NEW MEDIA

Although most of us imagine an Internet-based company runs from a noisy, haphazard environment designed on the fly with furniture on wheels and not a knot of wood to be found, Happy Boys and Girls—or HBG New Media—defies that perception. HBG New Media, a company founded in 1993 that creates information technology and commerce sites and businesses and Exponia, a popular online product used to promote trade shows, is a serene enclave of hushed tones, traditional furnishings, and wood walls throughout. The paradigm is that with all the traditional touches, a tour through the offices is far from a typical corporate headquarters, thanks to the design direction of Chicago-based firm Valerio Dewalt Train (VDT).

A COSMOS OF CREATIVITY

Led by David Jennerjahn of VDT, the interior of the 8,600-square-foot (799-square-meter) office feels and looks more like a hushed journey into a sacred, serene space somewhere in the outer stratosphere. Jennerjahn says that his client wanted to translate the random Web-surfing experience into a physical office space. But Jennerjahn manifested an interior that took its cues from the fortuitous patterns that tend to connect in cyberspace. HBG New Media's office follows a non-directional route where public spaces, meeting and presentation rooms, and staff departments each have a lounge, coined "a home page," but the areas are all arranged in a free-form, yet flowing manner, much like the act of surfing the Web. A journey through HBG New Media's office would almost mimic what it would be like if the visitor were free-floating through outer space, with touches of smoky blue walls, sandblasted glass partitions, columns of shimmery metal, and lights that look like twinkling stars.

"No matter how electronic your business may be, there's a physical element, too. Being innovative and successful is more than hiring the right people and buying the best technology. You've got to create a culture where space matters."

Tom Kelley, author and general manager, IDEO, *The Art of Innovation*

One of the common areas is the living room, a haven for employees who need a moment of cool, quiet peace. Blue upholstered chairs with chrome accents, plus surrounding sandblasted glass panels and a 13-foot-high (3.9-meter-high) exposed ceiling (up to the concrete grid), make the space seem larger and somewhat otherworldly. A digital projection television and beer taps in the living room complete the soothing moment.

In other areas of the office near workstations and meeting areas, spaces are more defined and intimate with segments of warm cherry or maple panels that form an L-shaped wall and attached ceiling canopy under the exposed concrete grid. Here, wall lights that look like brilliant stars reflect off of sandblasted glass wall panels.

TROPICAL PARADISE
DENT & COMPANY

People often want special objects in their offices, but not many have the chance to build a workspace filled with their passions. But when investment banker Stephen Dent moved his headquarters to a new space, he decided to surround himself with his passion for marine life. Austin Patterson Disston Architects, House of Fins, and Dent all worked together to find and implement the detailing to make this 7,500-square-foot office (697-square-meter) a tropical haven.

BUILDING A PASSIONATE OFFICE

The design concept evolved from the client's personal interest in marine life. As a young boy, Dent traveled to Hawaii and witnessed tropical fish in their natural habitat and fell in love with the beauty and grace of these exotic creatures. Over the years, he became a world-traveling scuba diver, and diving has become an all-consuming passion. He brought his passion home by installing a large tank in his house, then went on to add a 400-gallon fish tank in his former office. It was no wonder that when it came time to design his new office, Dent decided to create an entire headquarters around fish tanks rather than try to squeeze a few fish tanks into the workspace after the fact.

The space and all its architectural details are designed around four large tanks. There were the inevitable challenges of designing a space with oversized aquariums. For instance, the architects had to design an interior that would not fight, or fade, amongst the brightly lit, dramatic tanks. "The space needed a strong design, since the fish tanks are such a dominant element," says David Austin, AIA, of Austin Patterson Disston. Nautical imagery ties together the tanks and the client's extensive collection of signed marine watercolors painted by artist John McRae. Nature's colors thread throughout the space. The fabric and rug colors of greens and blues are derived from the colors of water in the tanks and the neutral wall covering throughout the space is grass-cloth. Especially nautical in theme are the wood panels under the tanks and around the furniture that evoke the feeling of being below deck on a luxury sailboat.

AN UNDERWATER PUZZLE

The second challenge was designing and installing the tanks. The window tank separating the small conference room and administrative area was specially crafted for the space. The other three saltwater tanks were assembled on site and all the heavy acrylic panels were crane-lifted through a window up to the office's third floor.

The House of Fins, the local aquarium retailer that designed, built, stocks, and maintains the tanks, carefully chooses the population of fish within each tank, so that they all get along. Dent's collection of over 200 species of fish, separated into appropriate tanks, includes toothy sharks, darting eels, and smaller, bright tropical fish, all of which are not on an endangered species list.

Dent wants to bring to other children what he experienced as a young boy when he discovered the underwater world. Groups of young schoolchildren can often be found taking tours of the office space since after all, Dent & Company's headquarters rivals the largest public aquariums of Norwalk and Mystic Seaport in Connecticut.

The largest tank, filled with predator fish, is 27 feet long, 4 feet wide, and 4 feet high (8.2 meters long by 1.2 meters wide by 1.2 meters high) and holds about 3,420 gallons of saltwater (in comparison, most freshwater tanks set up in homes hold 10 to 20 gallons of water). Work surfaces in the administrative areas are inlaid with Ubatuba granite and credenzas have inlays of Aquazul, the materials used to craft the compass in the entryway.

Dent's love of all things nautical is evident as soon as the elevator opens. There, a model yacht found at Mystic Seaport sits proudly illuminated and enclosed in glass. The floor design is a compass outlined by wood and brass strips and alternating Aquazul and Ubatuba granite and Crème Marfil and Tuscan Green marble.

"There's a domestic, soothing look to the space."
David Austin, Austin Patterson Disston Architects

Architect David Austin refers to the office's design as a modern interpretation of a quiet, elegant English library of all wood. The desks, bookcases, conference tables, and side tables were all designed by the architects. Furniture and wood paneling throughout the offices are made from cherry and ash burl, framed by a darker cherry.

SPECS
TANKS OF TRANQUILITY

Although there is a predator tank in Dent's office, most corporate clients prefer peaceful, slower-moving fish. One shark in the tank made a Dent employee a bit nervous before she became used to it. But for the most part, people who work in an environment filled with fish tanks are calmer, more relaxed because they are surrounded by water and nature. Why? According to the American Pet Products Manufacturers Association (APPMA), the soothing motion of vibrantly colored fish swimming mesmerizes and relaxes the viewer.

- A survey of 100 fish owners by the APPMA found that those with aquariums have lower blood pressure, suffer less from stress, sleep better, have a more successful personal life, and missed fewer days of work.
- A study showed that when adults watched an aquarium they experienced reduced blood pressure levels, according to an article in the *Psychiatric Times* (February 1999).
- A study of aquarium owners revealed a decrease in anxiety during mild to moderately stressful situations because of the calming, relaxing, stress-reducing effects of watching fish and inducing feelings of serenity (*The Journal of Nervous and Mental Disease*, 1991 and *Psychological Reports*, 1999).

DENT'S FISH LIST

Partial list of species in Dent's tanks (Dent's advice: Don't mix or add species without the help of an aquatic expert):

- Leopard shark
- Moray eels
- Firefish
- Filefish

- Nurse shark
- Golden trebolies
- Red hawkfish
- Clown triggers

- Black tip reef shark
- Yellow wrasse
- Pygmy angelfish
- Damsels

Behind three of the enormous tanks is a service room and storage center, much like an oversized closet, that holds all the equipment necessary to maintain the aquariums. The aquarium in the reception area can also be seen from the conference room through glass windows inserted in the door. The custom conference table is inlaid with Ubatuba and Aquazul granite and trimmed with wood to give this room an earthy feel from floor to ceiling.

> "There is nothing in a caterpillar that tells you it's going to be a butterfly."
> R. Buckminster Fuller, architect and inventor of the geodesic dome

SPACE FOR METAMORPHOSIS
NEXSPACE

Transitions can be daunting times. You're feeling neither here nor there, with no roots or home to speak of. Employees who are in a migratory state may feel confused, unfocused, and left without an identity. David Agger, founder of Nexspace, wanted to create a workspace that was non-traditional, contemporary, and collegial to meet the emotional and physical needs of mobile staffers; emerging companies, temporary project teams, displaced sales units, consultants, and out-of-town companies waiting to find a permanent space in the Los Angeles area. Agger felt that is was unproductive for companies to be bogged down with relocation problems, and that employees should be free to focus on core business activities.

AN EMERGING WORKFORCE

Agger commissioned Beckson Design Associates to create an appealing atmosphere for this new type of workforce. To appeal to the widest range of potential clients, it was necessary to accommodate individual workers, as well as larger groups coming together as a team in the space. The populations of occupants would range from younger groups to more established professionals, all who share a desire for flexible and functional workspace where they could still feel and be creative and productive though in temporary quarters.

The plan was to keep the 17,000-square-foot (1,579-square-meter) space simple and straightforward for new temporary tenants to immediately understand. The space has a central area where shared amenities are pooled (mail, copier, server room, concierge, on-site management, and main conference room). Blocks of development (or work) rooms are divided into small, medium, and large sizes modularly designed around mobile desks. The space fits thirty-nine companies, or 200 occupants, at a time.

WHERE EVERYONE KNOWS YOUR NAME

The comfortable, casual, and contemporary space is meant to feel like a campus meeting place, to foster workplace envy among those in permanent offices, says Agger. The 1,150-square-foot (107-square-meter) Center Quad,

or the living room/lounge area, is core to Nexspace's effort to help occupants combine work and leisure. Yet for more senior, established tenants, there are areas of more privacy. One of the offices, known as the "Delta Space," is triangular in shape and juts out dramatically from the building to give the occupant more than 60 feet (18 meters) of unobstructed views of downtown L.A., Catalina Island, and Malibu.

A HIP HOME

The idiosyncratic choices in furniture in the common areas play a large part in making tenants feel individual while at the same time feel like they are at home. There's no cookie-cutter approach to the design elements in the shared spaces. Each piece of furniture has its own personality, much like people do. To highlight the concept of distinct personalities coming together to share space, even the carpets were chosen for their own individual character rather than on how they might coordinate with accent walls or even with each other.

The space clearly celebrates independence, character, and how various—even colorful—personalities can express themselves and work together all under one roof.

Inner development rooms are pulled away from the west curtain wall to leave the view from the promenade open for all to enjoy. Reading areas along the promenade encourage occupants to gather in groups or sit in solitude for contemplation.

THE INSPIRED WORKSPACE   92

"Creative minds always have been known to survive any kind of bad training."
Anna Freud, child psychiatrist and daughter of Sigmund Freud

The central pod includes a lounge, dining hall, and café with residual spaces for personal escape. It's flooded with natural light and expands towards the curtain wall to maximize the distant ocean views. It's painted white to allow the diverse colors, personality, and textures of each of the pieces of the handpicked modern furniture—by designers including Alvar Aalto, Eames, George Nelson, and Karim Rashid—to come through.

"When working on ethereal challenges sometimes it's necessary to look at things in a different way — and your surroundings just might help." From the Nexspace Web site

The walls of the development rooms are built of translucent fiberglass reinforced plastic (FRP) to filter in natural light. The FRP also serves as floor-to-ceiling dry-marker board that is durable, easy to clean, and withstands any damage resulting in frequent use of short-term tenants. The doors are large, sliding, cell-structured FRP panels that are easy to open. Rooms are furnished with custom 30-inch by 48-inch (76-centimeters by 122-centimeters) mobile desks.

"First keep the peace within yourself, then you can also bring peace to others."
Thomas a` Kempis, German monk and religious scholar

The conference room is surrounded with a panel of Lexan that is gently curved. It is the common room where the group of six designers who work in the office often eat lunch together. Jazz can be heard throughout the office during the entire day; the spirited music combined with the tranquil setting is the perfect blend of inspiration for the designers.

BREATHING SPACE
TEXTILE/GRAPHIC DESIGN STUDIO

Once textile designer Lori Weitzner had the chance to find raw space for her studio, she grabbed it. Up until that point, Weitzner had shared studios with other designers. Although she always had the opportunity to decorate her space, she now finally had the chance to structurally create the one-of-a-kind studio that she always envisioned.

Weitzman decided to share the space with a long-time friend and colleague, graphic designer Jill Korostoff. Weitzner and Korostoff shared the same aesthetics—they both appreciated a clean, minimal look to their workspace. The search for a workplace began.

A CLEAR VISION

The designers found a 3,000-square-foot (279-square-meter) space that was "absolutely disgusting," Weitzner says. "If you didn't have a vision, you'd have walked right out of the space." She describes the old space as a field of cubicles and ugly blue carpet. But what appealed to the designers was the bank of windows on the north side of the building and the clear, open views of landmark buildings, such as the Empire State Building. They agreed to "get rid of everything" in the space, and start fresh with a big, empty rectangle.

Architect Peter Tow was hired to reconstruct the rental space on a tight budget. "Lori had an image in mind of what she wanted in the workspace," Tow says. "She verbally described what she wanted and how she wanted to feel in the space, and I knew she wanted a Zen-like workplace."

Weitzner remembers her wish list. "I wanted the space to be white, but not cold. I wanted as much daylight as possible, and I wanted the space to have an ethereal feel to it," she says. "I wanted it to be a haven from the streets of Manhattan." But the word that kept coming up for Weitzner was "watery." She loved the feel of water, the look of water. Weitzner realized the quality she loves about water is that it looks translucent, transparent, and opaque at the same time. Somehow, some way, Weitzner wanted Tow to translate that feeling into a tangible space.

The solution was to use ½-inch-thick (1.27-centimeter-thick) clear, ribbed Lexan panels to carve out space without obstructing light. The translucent panels run east and west to define space and filter light, while solid walls run north and south to provide privacy and separation. Each designer has a private office with sliding "screens," or doors made from Lexan panels.

"I can tell you that everyone that walks into this space says there is a great energy here," says Weitzner. "Everyone feels good here, the space makes all of us feel whole and refreshed."

The office is more like a blank canvas than finished piece of art. The designers decided they needed to be surrounded by a neutral palette so they could focus and create new designs that often use vivid color and busy pattern during the day. Anything but a white backdrop of a workspace would be overwhelming during the design process, Weitzner says.

Lexan walls face the windows so the light can stream in without obstruction. Most days, the office lights are off because so much natural daylight floods the space.

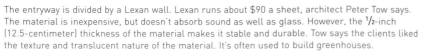

The entryway is divided by a Lexan wall. Lexan runs about $90 a sheet, architect Peter Tow says. The material is inexpensive, but doesn't absorb sound as well as glass. However, the 1/2-inch (12.5-centimeter) thickness of the material makes it stable and durable. Tow says the clients liked the texture and translucent nature of the material. It's often used to build greenhouses.

SPECS
ELEGANT LEXAN

Lexan, a polycarbonite developed by General Electric Structured Products and once viewed as a lowly plastic material, has come into its own as an alternative for glass, fiberglass, and PVC in construction. Other benefits of Lexan material include:

- It's non-yellowing.
- As a sheet it is easy to install (cut, drill, and screw) with simple woodworking tools.
- It's lightweight and tough and can be cold-formed to gentle curves.
- Clear Lexan transmits about 90 percent of light.
- It doesn't chip.

Tow used simple and painted 2 x 4 strips of wood as frames for the ribbed Lexan panels installed in the studio he designed. "The ribbed texture breaks up the light to create a shimmery effect, which is unique to the material," Tow says. "It lets light in while allowing a certain level of privacy. The images seen through the panels are broken up to create interesting effects, not unlike a fuzzy television image."

"The world is but a canvas to the imagination."
Henry David Thoreau, author and naturalist

Each designer has a private office. Lori Weitzner's office is specifically for paperwork and lounging around. There's another space where Weitzner does her designing, where she can drop huge bolts of fabric without getting in anyone's way.

"One of the advantages of being disorderly is that one is constantly making exciting discoveries." A.A. Milne, author

THE PLAYFUL WORKSPACE

WHERE PEOPLE WORK HARD AND PLAY HARD

A playful workspace is joyfully designed with fun and frolic in mind. The workspace is designed to help bring out the child within, to awaken employees' lighthearted nature, to help them recover their experiences of playtime. This particular work environment aims to remove barriers to creativity by building in toys that awaken the spirit and mind.

No employer can force fun on its employees but can encourage a playful attitude toward the work at hand. There's a time and a place for fun at work. The employees who are likely to benefit in a playful workspace are more conservative, introverted people who need a bit of fun now and then to help loosen things up at work. Those who are children at heart will have no trouble taking to a playful workspace. Extroverted people will naturally gravitate towards a fun work environment because it appeals to their desire to entertain and be entertained as a way of letting loose and bonding with others.

The following workspaces show play in action. They are friendly, amusing playgrounds in which to work out and solve business problems. The projects shown here are designed to reflect an energy and the imaginative nature of the corporate culture of the company. In some instances, the playful aspect is subtle, as with Brendan Moore &

Associates in Canada. Brendan Moore may at first seem like a calm place with its muted color palette, but look deeper and you will find a workspace that is specifically designed to make introverted employees feel and act a bit more extroverted, a strategy to help the company become spontaneous and bond better. Other companies featured are unabashed when it comes to showing the world how fun it is to work for them. PUSH, an ad agency in Florida, was founded by three young partners who created such an inspiring work environment inside and out that the building is now often mistaken by vacationers as a must-see tourist attraction in downtown Orlando.

A company with a playful bent to its work environment does not have to be in the entertainment or creative field. There are plenty of industries that could stand to have a bit of levity in the workplace—from a taxation firm to a company that specializes in machine imaging technology, there's no harm in having a little fun.

"You might just find that spirit of fun will push you toward designing a great new experience."
Tom Kelley, author *The Art of Innovation*, general manager of IDEO

"As the creative adult needs to toy with ideas, the child, to form his ideas, needs toys."
Bruno Bettelheim, child psychologist

Architect Heather Faulding raided her client's prop rooms to quickly and easily design the space. The laminate conference table was placed on top of a large, sturdy commercial ashtray column, then painted bright red to fit in with the décor. Walls stayed white, but the inside window sashes were accented with red or yellow paint to create a finished look without spending money on window treatments.

FUN ON A BUDGET
RINGLING BROTHERS

A retailing venture for the renowned circus company led to the development of a buyer's office in Manhattan. A low budget and six weeks to complete the project meant that architect Heather Faulding needed to be inventive in designing the interior of this 4,000-square-foot (372-square-meter) space.

THE SPIRIT OF A COMPANY

"Whenever I do a showroom, it's as important as the store design," Faulding says. "You immediately have to get into the spirit of what the product is—that's the number one objective." Faulding's client wanted the office to have all the fun of a circus, but designed in a way that was clearly professional, as well.

Faulding and her client raided the company's prop rooms to find design elements. "There were wonderful elephant blankets and horse-riding props that we took and hung or propped in corners," Faulding says.

Although Faulding wishes more companies would be willing to take risks in the design of workspaces, she does believe that the dot.com industry had a large influence on the work environment. "But not enough to push the envelope," she says. "I wish people could understand that their offices can have a large degree of individuality, rather than being boring and traditional."

The carpeting came from remnants of a custom design used in the Ringling Brothers retail stores. The chairs were quickly upholstered in red and blue fabric, accented with tassels to add to the party feeling in the office space.

"No one in today's offices dresses like they are in straitjackets anymore."
Heather Faulding, architect

CREATURE COMFORTS
MONSTER.COM

It's an Internet venture that's still strong and kicking since its launch in 1994, especially in the roller-coaster economy that thrust throngs of job seekers out into the real world. Monster.com, now a global network that connects career seekers and progressive companies looking to recruit, has language sites in the United Kingdom, Australia, Hong Kong, France, and India, to name a few countries. It was also the official online career management services sponsor of the 2002 Olympic Winter Games and 2002 and 2004 U.S. Olympic Teams. New from Monster.com is the creation of Monster Office HQ, an online source with Web-based tools that acts as a center for employers in need of managing the hiring process. No doubt, the once deemed unconventional recruitment company is keeping creative, due in part, to the crazy workplace founder Jeff Taylor created.

MAKING WORK FUN

Taylor's management philosophy is simple: He believes that it is up to a company leader to make work fun. From the giant statue of his company's 10-foot-high (3-meter-high) green and purple monster mascot, called Trump, in the lobby to the frat house-like employee parties, Taylor has created a work-hard, play-hard atmosphere that entices many employees, and maddens others who have left because they felt the workplace was less than professional. Taylor's critics feel he's gone too far with his antics; others are proud enough to bring in their families and friends to tour the office.

The company's 75,000-square-foot (6,968-square-meter) workplace takes up one floor in a former nineteenth-century textile mill in New England. Taylor founded the company in an office above a bowling alley and Chinese restaurant, then put sales reps in trailers to accommodate the company's explosive growth. Through this experience, Taylor quickly learned what he envisioned as an ideal work setting for his company.

It's not only a new company, it's a youthful one. Kahler Slater, a Milwaukee-based architecture firm, was hired to help Monster.com become the workplace Taylor envisioned. After numerous employee interviews, it was clear to the design firm that the office would be colorful to reflect the company's corporate culture.

COLLEGIAL INSPIRATION AND INPUT

Since Monster.com has a large call center full of sales representatives fielding calls from clients, that group was housed on one end of the floor far from external distractions such as the reception area and team rooms. The result: A workplace where employees meet up with each other frequently, without negotiating elevators, stairs, or floors that tend to divide workers, rather than unite them.

The goal of making the office the most technologically advanced, interactive, and fun workspace in the country seems to work, even in uncertain dot.com times. The company continues to thrive and redefine the standard for online hiring management solutions by branching out and bringing out new products for human resources professionals, proving once again that a fun, colorful workspace can inspire serious, cutting-edge thinkers.

"If a man does not keep pace with his companions, perhaps it is because he hears a different drummer. Let him step to the music which he hears, however measured or far away."
Henry David Thoreau, author and naturalist

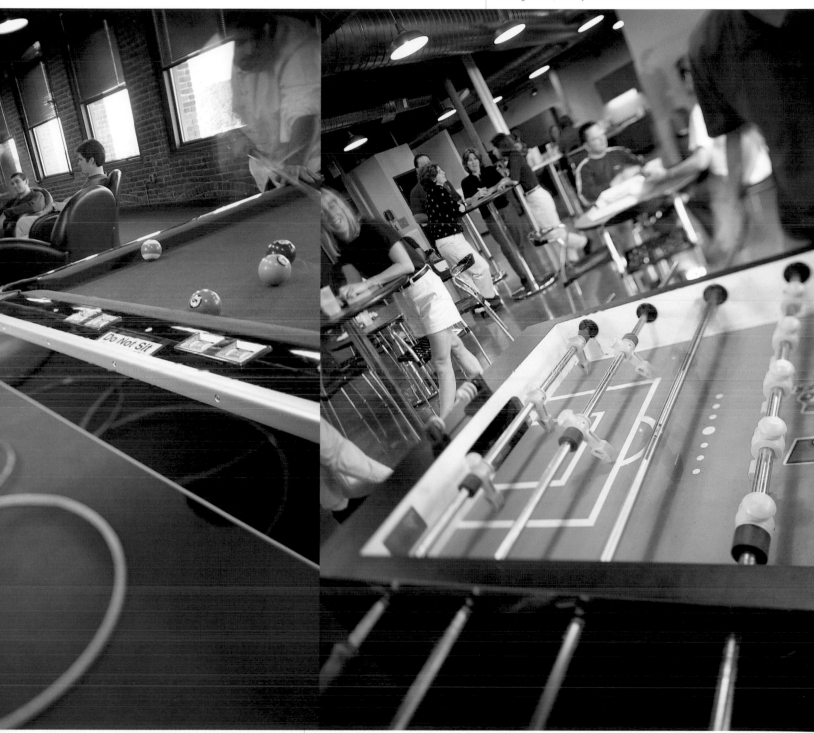

Monster.com founder Jeff Taylor believes in putting levity into the workday, as evidenced by the workspace. Bright colors, game rooms, and café settings help define and enhance the energy and fun of the culture. The most-used setting is the Monster Den, where employees gather for meetings on oversized armchairs.

"People only see what they are prepared to see." Ralph Waldo Emerson, poet and essayist

The stainless-steel façade of PUSH's new building never has to be polished, and it holds up well in Florida's humidity and rain. There's no maintenance, and the effect looks like a brilliant stainless-steel kitchen sink. But to be on the safe side, seams were caulked, then covered with waterproofing tape.

CAUSING A STIR
PUSH ADVERTISING AGENCY

You know your workspace is irresistible when your client moves in with you. That's what happened to PUSH, the ad agency in Orlando, when one of its clients, a man who worked for a major corporation filled with traditional blond wood furniture and white walls, set up shop in the blueberry-colored conference room twice a week because he felt energized there. Founders Julio Lima, Richard Wahl, and John Ludwig were honored by their client's constant and reassuring presence, but they sorely needed the space for team project work.

TRYING TO STAY INSPIRED

Space wasn't the only issue PUSH grappled with in the old warehouse they leased. The founding partners came together in 1996 and suddenly found themselves growing by leaps and bounds, adding client after client, project after project. But trying to stay focused and inspired became too difficult while crunched together in 2,000 square feet (189 square meters) of confining space with vents that bordered a smoke-filled, loud, country-western bar next door. The workplace became a mishmash of spaces that were arranged haphazardly to accommodate new account teams, and the mechanical bull in the bar's parking lot was getting to be a bit too annoying. After scouting for new space, the partners decided to build a headquarters on an empty lot in a mixed-use area of downtown Orlando.

RELIEF...AND FAME

The partners hired The Evans Group—an architectural firm with an inspiring workplace of its own—to design the PUSH building. One night, Leonard Feinberg from The Evans Group put two and two together and came up with a design for the building based on the company's metal business cards. The idea for the metal façade was born, a sculptor whose specialty is stainless steel and has some background in construction was hired, and the 6,000-square-foot (540-square-meter), one-story star of the neighborhood was born.

The partners worried how the neighborhood and the conservative downtown development council would take to such a shiny structure surrounded by the traditional local fare of stucco and brick buildings. It was needless anxiety. The Ernestine Street building is often mistaken for a tourist attraction. PUSH is often written up in local magazines as "one site to see in Orlando". The building is used as a backdrop in TV and print spots, tour buses stop in for a spin around the building, and one romantic man tends to bring his dates to see the building, champagne in hand.

"People ask how we feel about the building. Our clients see the building expect big things from us. So, it's been a friend to us. It's helped us to set the bar higher on our own creativity." John Ludwig, founder of PUSH

Back in the old building, the team painted its conference room this same lush, rich Caribbean blue, which happened to be the corporate color of a client the company was pitching. The result: PUSH won the account, so the color is considered to be a good luck charm, which they decided to use in the new building. Though the ceiling throughout the building is exposed, large swags of heavy fabric curtains will be hung in the conference room to absorb echoes and soften the acoustics in the room without structurally changing the space.

There are only a couple of private offices in the building, but they don't feel boxy because the ceilings are open and no one shuts their door during the day. Every one of the company's thirty employees is encouraged to decorate their own office or workspace according to personal passions. One account executive found plush, colorful chairs that look like women's shoes and brought them into her open workspace. Here, founder John Ludwig's office has bright walls. The painters hated the job, Ludwig says, because it took nearly a dozen coats of paint to drench the drywall for the saturated color the partners envisioned.

ENDING EMPLOYEE ISOLATION

"We have no disgruntled employees," says Julio Lima, a founding partner of PUSH. "Our turnover rate is low because we've created a place where we'd like to work as an employee."

The partners of PUSH chalk up the low turnover rate to the corporate culture they've created—one of inclusion. The company has doubled its size each year, losing only one or two employees a year due to a spousal transfer, a move to another state, or a desire to change fields or go back to school.

When the partners formed PUSH in 1996, they drew up a checklist of good and bad things about the places in which they worked, and they tried to eliminate as many things in the "bad" column as possible. "There are lots of barriers in agencies, both physical and emotional," partner John Ludwig says. "We wanted to create a workplace with no real or perceived walls." The partners did notice that the more walls they erected in the workspace, the less idea generation happened. That was because people stayed behind their desks, behind their four walls, and there was no longer a cross-pollination of ideas. Instead of cowering in cubicles, the partners wanted to get employees out of their comfort zones and mingle.

It has worked beautifully, they say. In fact, they describe one success story. The company's junior production manager was isolated behind walls in the old building, and he had a disjointed sense of the company's philosophies and creative processes. He used to ask to be part of the creative process. But now, he's sitting center stage and aware of every job that comes and goes, and is better able to track the process. "He's more creative now, too, because he's not isolated," Ludwig says. "He's part of the creative solution, the idea generation, and he's always offering concepts we actively embrace."

"You miss 100 percent of the shots you never take."

Wayne Gretzky, professional hockey player

Colors were carefully considered throughout the building. The use of yellow was an outgrowth from their old space, says Julio Lima, the partner who chose the colors. "Yellow is energizing. It wakes you up in the morning, but it's not such a bold hue that it blinds you," he adds. The blues and greens around the other parts of the office balance and soothe the eye.

"You need chaos in your soul to give birth to a dancing star."
Friederich Nietzsche, German philosopher

In the early days of the agency's history, basketball games were numerous. Now, the teams are too busy for daily tryouts. But it's common to see bright blue "stress balls" flying around from workstation to workstation to relieve some stress.

Earth Treks Inc.'s office has an attached gym in the form of an indoor climbing center. The successful professional-guide service in Columbia, Maryland, has a well-used climbing center that is 15,000 square feet (1,394 square meters) in size and 44 feet high (13.4 meters high). The center has the ability to host parties and offers climbing lessons to drive business to the company's locale. There's a big perk for working there. Every employee gets free membership to the gym to perfect his or her rock-climbing capabilities—and to let off a little steam now and again.

PEAK OF PRODUCTIVITY

If you or your client want something slightly different in a workspace to get employees feeling physical, try an artificial indoor climbing wall.

Climbing walls are typically computer-generated designs built by specialty companies that understand the expertise levels and weight-bearing issues of such a large, but serious, toy. According to the Climbing Wall Industry Group, there are written specifications available for the design and building of artificial walls.

Most climbing walls are created out of existing cinder block walls, or made from plywood panels attached to walls and covered in a special textured material, then finished by inserting anchors. Options are unlimited, and designers of walls can create rounded corners, cracks, slabs, roofs, overhangs, anything that simulates a rock-climbing route. Depending on the complexity of the design, most walls cost less than $100 per square foot. Just don't forget to install soft flooring for easy landings!

The lobby is painted "PUSH green," the partners say. "It's the color of our logo. It's our signature color, so we wanted to use it for our first impression," Richard Wahl, one of the three partners at PUSH says. "We didn't want to overdo it, either, but we wanted to use the chartreuse because green is the color of moving forward, and of prosperity."

"Our passion for productivity increasingly depends upon the productivity of our passions."

Michael Schrage, author, co-director of MIT Media Lab

PLAYING FOR PROFITS
COGNEX CORPORATION

These days, it seems every company has a foosball table in their offices, including Cognex, a company founded in 1981 that specializes in image-analysis hardware and software used by semiconductor and electronics companies. But Cognex's playtime goes beyond foosball.

WHO ARE YOU CALLING A COGNOID?

Work at Cognex, and you'll be called a Cognoid, but in return, you have the benefit of a fitness center, onsite cafeteria, and a game room open twenty-four/seven to employees, friends, and family. In addition, 300 Cognoids in the 100,000-square-foot (9,290-square-meter) corporate headquarters (there are about 700 Cognoids worldwide) have chance to play ultimate Frisbee at noon in the athletic field next door and are encouraged to unabashedly celebrate Halloween, the company's official holiday when everyone comes to work in costume to win prizes. It doesn't end there. Cognoids can take a "night off" every other month when the company rents out a local movie theater for employees and their guest. The list of Cognex perks is long, and the workplace is fun—and it's not accidental.

MANAGEMENT'S SENSE OF HUMOR

Founder and President, CEO, and Chairman Dr. Robert J. Shillman has always had a sense of humor, starting when he kicked off the company's first dental plan in the early 1980s by handing out toothbrushes and toothpaste to employees at a company meeting. It's grown from four employees to hundreds, and as the company has grown, it's been a challenge to keep the fun corporate culture alive and intact while overcoming competition in the machine-visioning market.

Cognex, known today as a market leader focused on an innovative business strategy, relies on employee dedication to keep its position in the industry. It has to. Competition in the machine-visioning industry has flourished, job-hopping is common in Boston—a haven for machine-visioning engineers—and employees work long days and into the nights to keep the company's cutting-edge mentality. And, the company has seen its rounds of layoffs during slumping sales. But management realizes that if a Cognex employee isn't treated well, that employee won't muster the necessary company dedication. And though Cognex has earned a chuckle or two over the years for its amusing corporate culture, it also gets kudos from Wall Street for creating a successful identity, even in the staid investment community.

"Fun: We work hard, and we play hard. We celebrate often to recognize our accomplishments and to motivate ourselves to achieve even higher levels of success in the future." Cognex Web site, #10 under 10 Core Values and Mission Statement

The Cognex game room features four pinball machines, a ping-pong table, table hockey, and foosball. It is open twenty hours a day, seven days a week, and is available to Cognoids whenever they need to take a break from work. A fitness room is equipped with treadmills, universal gym, life cycles, NordikTrak, and free weights. Like the game room, the fitness room is open twenty-four hours a day, seven days a week.

"The more I give myself permission to live in the moment and enjoy it without feeling guilty...the better I feel about the quality of my work." Wayne Dyer, author

The executives at Brendan Moore have extensive experience at other traditional accounting firms. That's precisely why the details and colors of this office are unique from those of other tax professionals, including the boardroom, which opens with a large metal sliding door. Metal details were used frequently in the space as a way to show that the firm is cutting-edge. Metal, however, is merged with subdued sage green wall paint and upholstery to exhibit a sense of prosperity, as well.

LOOSENING UP
BRENDAN MOORE & ASSOCIATES

You might expect the typical tax and accounting professionals' office to be filled with private offices along the window, all wood case goods, and upholstered furnishings and carpet in classic colors like basic burgundy and navy. But that's not what Brendan Moore & Associates, a group of young sales tax management professionals who came from various traditional accounting firms, wanted for their new offices. Brendan Moore, the youngest of the group, runs the company and wanted to create a workspace that was "less conventional than the typical accountant type office."

EMBRACING INTROVERTED EMPLOYEES

In response, the design firm of Comley Van Brussel created a space incorporating elements that make for a playful, but serious and solid, tax management office. The company's corporate brochure, using smart colors and cutting-edge graphics, drove the design firm's use of shape and color in the 3,425-square-foot (318-square-meter) space.

Their desire to be viewed as a leading-edge, yet solid and stable company was exhibited in the use of metal materials, such as doors, stools, and lighting fixtures to give spark among the warmth of cherry veneer office suites and boardroom furniture.

Much of the office is open plan, using Herman Miller's Resolve workstations with screens printed with the firm's signature green. The designers paid special attention to the kitchenette area—which turns into a bistro and wine area after hours—because it was intended to promote interaction between the staff who otherwise are a bit introverted.

"They have beer and pizza afternoons," says Kathy van Brussel, leading designer on the project. "They are expanding into space downstairs that will be a mirror image of this space, but it was tough to get anyone to move out of the existing space because they don't want to be far from the fun."

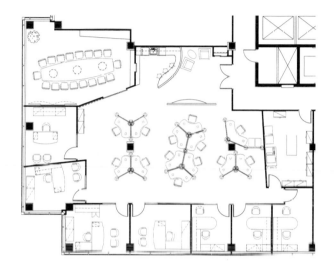

"If you focus on results, you will never change. If you focus on change, you will get results." Jack Dixon, biologist

Designer Kathy van Brussel says the kitchen was one of the most important parts of this design. Since employees in a tax management office can be introverted, it was important to have an inviting area near the front of the office where co-workers felt comfortable enough to mingle during the day and after hours. Cabinets in the bistro area are stocked with gourmet coffees and treats especially for employees. The bar is curved to match the walls and the metal stools and light fixtures bring more modern elements into the tax offices.

The client did not want an office filled with traditional square cubicles and straight walls. Curved and angled multitone surfaces, called accent walls, were used as a way to convey a sense of surprise in the space. Sage walls match the Herman Miller Resolve workstation screens. Burnt orange is used as another accent color on walls. A few of the walls double as privacy panels for workstations, and the café area, as well. The mix of flooring materials, colors, and patterns are unexpected and curved like the walls.

"Thank goodness I was never sent to school; it would have rubbed off some of the originality."
Beatrix Potter, English author and illustrator, *The Tale of Peter Rabbit*

The third floor of the schoolhouse is dedicated to the Corey McPherson Nash studio, which specializes in strategic print and interactive design for a variety of clients in technology and professional services. That space differs from the floor below in that it is more elegant and subdued, though far from conservative. A graceful, undulating, yellow wall, blond hardwood floors, and touches of metal design elements show the creative, cutting-edge side of that division.

Garage doors painted in primary colors like blue and yellow can be found throughout the Big Blue Dot's second-floor workspace. Understanding kids' culture is what they do, so toys of all sorts—that adults play with—rule the space. It's often described as "Peewee's Playhouse," but if you remember the movie *Big*, with Tom Hanks, you'll get a good idea of what goes on in this space.

"You get a sense that this is a fun place to work; its lively spirit is played out in the interior spaces."
Andrea Naddaff, partner, Corey & Company

SCHOOL OF FUN ARTS
COREY & COMPANY

When a company grows, it sometimes outgrows the often-odd workspace it started in and moves into a more traditional office environment. Tom Corey, founder of Corey & Company, did just the opposite and moved his expanding but splintered company (studios were located in disjointed spaces) into one quirky, offbeat building.

When the now-deceased founder of the company went on a hunt for space for his design studios, he made it a point to look at unconventional types of buildings like garages and schoolhouses. "The reason these types of spaces interested Tom was because he believed in working in a creative environment that would be inspiring and let people feel like they could work outside of the box," Andrea Naddaff, partner with Corey & Company, says.

A PLACE TO LIVE AND LEARN

The schoolhouse concept won out when Corey found a renovated four-story brick Catholic school for the three studios that fall under parent company Corey & Company. There was more than enough room for Corey McPherson Nash, Big Blue Dot, and Hatmaker—each studio having a vastly different corporate culture, specialty, and clientele roster that ranges from Cinemax, Nickelodeon, and Disney, to Harvard University. But all three studios co-exist quite peacefully—or playfully—on two floors of the converted schoolhouse (other companies occupy the first and fourth floors).

The company may be in a school, but look what a creative school they've turned it into! The interiors are colorful, but classic at the same time. From the yellow-and-cornflower-blue Corey McPherson Nash workspaces to the brightly stenciled floors in Big Blue Dot's area, bright, vivid color ties together the company's varied offices. "We needed to appeal to our corporate clientele, but at the same time we didn't want the space to be conservative," Naddaff says. Many of the architectural elements of the schoolhouse stayed as is. "We kept the bathrooms where they were, the old wooden floors, and the concave walls of the school,

but we tore out the dilapidated gym." Many of the original windows have stayed, too. To maximize the light streaming in from the oversized schoolhouse windows, interior walls were fitted with double-hung windows while others were constructed from corrugated translucent plastic.

SCHOOL WAS NEVER SO MUCH FUN

When the company moved into the schoolhouse, the intent was to give each creative team the opportunity to design its own space by deciding what the layout would be, where people would sit, and colors that would identify the essence of the studio. The result? Corey McPherson Nash, the original studio that develops print and interactive communications for clients in need of branding and corporate identity, has a more sophisticated color palette, Big Blue Dot, the studio that produces print and new-media design for children, looks like a playhouse filled with toys and Crayola colors. Hatmaker, specializing in broadcast design, has a space that expresses itself through vivid colors. There's one large conference area to accommodate the entire Corey & Company staff that's located in Big Blue Dot's office space and accessible through an electric-blue garage door.

The buzz about the company's workspace began in 1999 when *Boston Magazine* picked Corey & Company as one of the seventy best places to work in the Boston area. The article stressed thoughtful design plays a critical role in a company's productivity and creativity, citing Corey & Company as a prime example of how even a joyful office with a blue tricycle hanging from the ceiling can translate into a profitable business.

The main entrance for all three companies is on the building's third floor, accessible by elevator, which was added when the schoolhouse was renovated. Stairways at either end of the building help everyone stay linked. Though the studios work independently of one another, they do stay connected by taking turns on a monthly basis to host company-wide design meetings and by collaborating on projects.

"Your sacred space is where you can find yourself again and again."
Joseph Campbell, American author, mythologist

Not everyone can work in an aqua office. But artists-at-heart crave large doses of color in their workspaces to help them feel unconventional and unorthodox in order to be creative.

THE **ARTISTIC** WORKSPACE

WHERE PEOPLE ARE SURROUNDED BY ELEMENTS OF ART

"The artist brain cannot be reached—or triggered—effectively by words alone.
The artist brain is the sensory brain—sight and sound, smell and taste, touch."

Julia Cameron, author, *The Artist's Way*

The artistic workspace is designed to help workers feel the freedom to unlock their creative abilities and ambitions in whatever form their art takes. An artistic workspace can be a studio for one or a corporate campus for hundreds. The size of the workspace is immaterial; the number of workers irrelevant. What matters is that the artistic environment is filled with symbols, color, and images meant to stimulate and engage the imagination and the senses. The result is a workplace where people understand that they can render their work and personal lives in richer and more vibrant colors than they ever before imagined.

The artistic workspace becomes a genuine expression of the inhabitant's personality and talents. Artists can't work in anything other than an environment that promises to open their minds and spirits to their creative nature. Those who inhabit artistic workplaces don't rely on formulas or buzzwords to design these unique spaces. Instead, they prefer to offer one-of-a-kind spaces that reflect, and respect, one-of-a-kind employees.

The following artistic workspaces are as unique as the individuals who work in them. In order to feel relaxed and in touch with his passion, photographer Eric Roth in Massachusetts has surrounded himself with objects that remind him of his cherished art: photography. Wieden + Kennedy's art-saturated headquarters in Oregon helps its people lead creative lives. And the walls of a former warehouse in Minnesota speak out to its employees and visitors through the use of art, poetry, and words that comfort and inspire. From sole studio to open workspace, artistic vision has a place in the creative workplace.

"A barn shall harbour heaven, a stall become a shrine." Richard Wilbur. poet

STABLE WORK
ERIC ROTH'S PHOTO STUDIO/BARN

While working out of an old factory loft space in Boston, Eric Roth made a name for himself as a sought-after interiors and food photographer for the likes of L.L. Bean, *Boston Magazine*, and *Domain*. But as Boston became more crowded, Roth's working environment began to inhibit, rather than inspire, him. Roth felt that his work life was becoming increasingly stressful and "anti-nurturing" as the commute became tiresome, the freight elevator to his studio was always broken down, and parking for his clients became a problem.

RESCUING A WRECK

The solution became clear—a move out of the city and into a more relaxed and rural setting. Roth and his wife eyed a house built in 1790—he loved the barn; she loved the yard. Although the barn was considered by Roth to be a wreck— the roof sagged and leaked and the floor was smashed concrete—he saw that it had more than enough potential to become his new photography studio and office. The result of Roth's vision is a workspace filled with artistic pleasures and authentic parts of his personality that honestly reflect his passion for photography.

Over three years, Roth worked to renovate the barn that was originally a two-story-high carriage house. The downstairs was once divided into four or five large bays to house carriages and horses. The upstairs was filled with grain bins, areas to stack hay, and shoots to shovel the food down to the horses below.

Roth acted as his own designer and worked with an architect on the technical aspects of the renovation, such as making sure the roof was in sturdy condition. The interior renovation work involved insulating walls, adding plumbing and electricity, and then removing nearly half of the second floor. The original 9-foot-high (2.7-meter-high) ceilings were still too low for Roth, who needs to place lights high in order to get the right effect during a shoot. By eliminating half of the second floor, the barn was given an airy, lofty, and more spacious feeling, as well.

The downstairs is approximately 1,500 square feet (139 square meters) and houses studio, workshop, basketball hoop, kitchen, and bath (behind the gas pump). The second floor, measuring 500 square feet (46 square meters), holds the administrative area where Roth's studio manager and assistant work. Roth added two skylights over each desk for additional natural light. To furnish the studio and office, Roth was given a 10-foot-high (3-meter-high) church vestment cabinet and roomy antique pharmacist's cabinet for storage, plus a vintage schoolteacher's desk for the upstairs workspace.

After the barn renovation was completed, Roth admits that it took him time to get used to the pastoral setting as a professional workplace. He's able to think more clearly, now that the distractions and frustrations of the city are behind him. In the winter, even his kids hold their birthday parties in the studio because the barn is designed inside and out to hold up under even the toughest conditions.

"Even my clients are more relaxed and comfortable when they're here for a shoot." Eric Roth

Roth left the exterior architecture of the eighteenth-century barn as he found it, adding only a fresh coat of paint. An addition was made to the barn in 1850.

The comfortable kitchen is the hub of the studio, illuminated by an antique red gas pump that runs on a cool-burning five-watt bulb. The pine floor, finished with three coats of polyurethane, is soft, warm, and quiet underfoot. Roth doesn't mind the dents in the floor because they add character to the workspace, plus, it's easy on the feet when he and his clients shoot a few hoops after a long day behind the lens.

"The studio, a room to which the artist consigns himself for life, is naturally important, not only as workplace, but also as a source of inspiration. And it usually manages, one way or another, to turn up in his product."

Grace Glueck, reporter and art critic, *The New York Times*

Roth tore down beadboard from the original second-floor ceiling, then recycled it as material for the upper part of the office walls, leaving it natural with a coat of varnish. Simple rough-planed pine planks for the bottom half of the wall are painted semi-gloss white.

MATERIALS FOR RUSTIC-STYLE WORKSPACES

- #4 pine for flooring
- beadboard for walls and ceiling
- rough-planed pine planks for walls
- vintage furniture and collectibles

BEST BARN ARCHITECTURE RESOURCES

- The Old Barn Journal: www.thebarnjournal.org
- Maintaining old barns: Vermont Division for Historic Preservation and Vermont Housing and Conservation Board, Montpelier, Vermont: www.uvm.edu/~vhnet/hpres/publ/barnb/bbtit.html.

COLOR: THE COMFORTS OF BARN RED

Red is often thought of an aggressive color that evokes anger and passion. Red, in varying doses, is a good color for an office where employees need to have continuous high levels of energy and where snap decisions must be made. For slower-paced offices, a muted mid-tone can be used successfully to create a softer, gentle work environment. From barn reds to berry, reds are all considered restful, traditional tints that are neither overly feminine nor masculine. Photographer Eric Roth has a red theme throughout his photographic studio, punctuated by a fire-engine-red gas pump.

A peaceful nook with books and a comfortable red-plaid upholstered chair and ottoman welcomes clients who want to unwind on shoots. Roth often takes breaks there, too, to read photography books and tinker with his vintage camera collection.

TOWER OF POWER
PILL MAHARAM ARCHITECTS STUDIO

Another word for "cube" is "block." That's how architect David Pill felt when he worked in a cubicle years ago. "It was hard to let go in that workspace. There was a stiffness in that type of office environment. It was repressive," Pill remembers. He soon found that working on the third floor of his home wasn't much better. He became claustrophobic—the roof of the top floor was sloped, so Pill felt closed in, snuffing out his creativity.

But there was hope. Pill and his wife, Hillary Maharam, a former landscape architect and current design journalist, bought their 1711 farmhouse with an outbuilding/garage just 90 feet (27 meters) away from the main house, with the intent of turning it into a studio for the architect.

Pill always believed that the best of architecture made a building fit into a site—a way to connect with nature—and was happy to have the chance to do that when designing his own studio. He also felt strongly that architecture should be "inventive and reflect what comes from within you." So he relied on his own instincts, his love of sustainable design, and astronomy to build an artistic haven that he dreamed about for so long.

CONNECTING WITH NATURE'S BEAUTY

In designing the studio in the two-story outbuilding, Pill knew he would create a central place where he could pursue all of his interests. So he included a workshop/sculpture studio downstairs, an architectural/art studio upstairs, and an observation tower on the side of the building as a perch for his telescope, and a way to stay connected to the creative and artistic inspirations he finds in nature's beauty. The studio is also a way to stay connected to his young children Jake and Liza, who visit dad during the day.

The dilapidated garage, snuggled into a hillside, was already in the perfect spot. Pill wrapped the exterior in corrugated metal and natural shingles, and topped it with a corrugated metal roof. Pill gutted the building's interior but kept the

original floor plan, adding only a bath and kitchenette behind a butter-cream-yellow painted wall, and raised the roofline slightly to create an airy, sun-filled, and uncluttered atelier.

The mix of sustainable materials further reflects Pill's love of nature. Custom-built cabinetry of birch and maple topped with slate line the southern wall of windows, radiant-tube heating covered by 4-by-8-foot (1.2-by-2.4-meter) sheets of Resindek—a formaldehyde-free particle board used for warehouse floors, rejuvenated timber collar ties, water-based wall paint, and ceiling fans—all promote a healthy, and inspiring, environment.

The 25-foot-tall (7.6-meter-tall) observation tower with two platforms is made of rough-hewn timbers. Architect David Pill built it to accommodate his love of astronomy. One year, the family gathered on the platform at 4 A.M. to watch a meteor shower; the next summer, a bird nested in the ladder—the architects watched the birthing process unfold through a tiny window on the doorway next to the doorknob (a great height for curious kids).

The unorthodox, nearly chartreuse–colored front door to the studio, designed by Pill and built by Kevin Whitney of Thomas Buckborough and Associates, speaks volumes of the architect's creativity. Rough-hewn slate steps offer a spot of warmth.

Pill wants to experiment more with sustainable materials, and has begun the process in his studio. He built a slate countertop under the bank of windows as a measure to build up thermal mass, using nature as a way to heat the space. For additional and even heat, Pill used a radiant heated floor, called Resindek, that looks and feels like cork when the tiles are turned upside down.

Even the walls of Pill's studio are uncluttered. As for color, Pill preferred to keep the interior walls clean and bright white, with the exception of one wall painted Pratt & Lambert's "Gladsome" #1713, a serene hue of butter yellow. Above, a simple sculptural touch— metal tie rods on the ceilin

SPECS
THE COST OF CLUTTER

Architect David Pill specifically designed an uncluttered workspace. "Clutter drives me crazy," he says. Pill admits to being neat and orderly, but admits that a too sterile environment makes him feel like he's not working. So, he's struck a balance, often keeping models on the countertop under the window, and filling the conference table with drawings of projects on tracing paper.

Even the furniture in Pill's studio is uncomplicated. The clean aluminum-frame conference table with glass top and straight-edged but colorful chairs form the common space in the atelier. The simple hanging pendant lighting hangs in the air without obstructing views. He even did away with intrusive baseboards and used radiant heated flooring, instead.

"...without clutter to obscure your vision, you will see more clearly..."
Michelle Passoff, author, *Lighten Up!*
Free Yourself from Clutter

"I feel that art has something to do with the achievement of stillness in the midst of chaos. I think that art has something to do with an arrest of attention in the midst of distraction." Saul Bellow, author

The Portland Institute for Contemporary Art (PICA), an avant-garde arts organization focused on promoting overlooked art and artists, is headquartered in Wieden + Kennedy's building. The Wieden + Kennedy space became a gallery of art for PICA and an inspiration for employees.

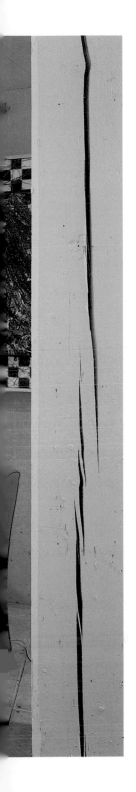

SPONTANEOUS COMBUSTION
WIEDEN + KENNEDY

Innovation is rarely found in a vacuum, but instead discovered when differing populations collide and mix to create something new and untested. Dan Wieden, founder of the ad agency Wieden + Kennedy, felt in his heart and soul that building an enclave for creative spirits in all shapes, sizes, and ages would be grand fodder for new ideas.

The agency, founded in 1982, opened its doors with one little-known client named Nike, and quickly grew to over 400 employees worldwide with offices in New York, Amsterdam, London, and Tokyo. Finally it outgrew its original location, and decided to create an innovative workspace that revolved around art in all its glorious forms.

"A great building not only changes your environment, it changes your outlook, your fortunes, your sense of self and community." Dan Wieden, co-founder of Wieden + Kennedy

WHERE BUSINESS MEETS ART

Wieden + Kennedy's new headquarters is the realization of co-founder Dan Wieden's goal to build a creative institution, a synergistic hub where business, art, and community thrive under one roof. To achieve this goal, Wieden collaborated with two Portland creatives: Brad Cloepfil, an emerging architect and founder of Allied Works Architecture, and Kristy Edmunds, Executive Director and Curator, Portland Institute for Contemporary Art (PICA) to build the inspired working village he envisioned.

Wieden found an abandoned circa 1914 icehouse that took up one entire block located in the heart of Portland's Pearl District, an industrial section of town that is home to artists, galleries, and boutiques. The open, loft-like space had an industrial energy to it, yet the design team could see that it was also a place that could be transformed into a new work dynamic, an environment where both fine art and commercial art could prosper. The main attraction to Wieden was the building's huge central atrium, which he envisioned would instigate spontaneous conversations between his agency's 250 Portland-based employees and artists who would be invited to share the same space. Wieden visualized more than just a well-designed workspace in an artists' enclave. His goal was to construct an environment that would foster creativity by building in easy opportunities for employees and community members to interact with the arts on a daily, if not hourly, basis.

INVITING IN THE MUSE

To do that, Wieden invited PICA to become the cornerstone tenant of his agency's new headquarters. He thought that with PICA in the building, employees would have casual chances to interact with fine arts on a daily basis by viewing exhibits in the gallery, watching performances in the amphitheater, or walking among "artists in residence" working in the atrium.

PICA now occupies 8,000 square feet (743 square meters) on the second floor including new offices, a 2,000-square-foot (186-square-meter) educational resource center and more than 2,200 square feet (204 square meters) of gallery space. The gallery and resource center are open to the public. PICA has access to the 400-seat amphitheater, which is the centerpiece of the building's new atrium.

The building's atrium, a dramatic five-story concrete structure, creates a sense of civic identity for the agency by serving as a cultural gathering place as well as the agency's spiritual core. This central piazza, which filters its way to the far reaches of the building via interior walkways and an open design, is a 20,000-square-foot (1,858-square-meter) area that includes the amphitheater, a screening room, and a gym. The building's sixth floor penthouse has a café, an outdoor terrace, and a state-of-the-art reference library. On the street level, the building has 22,000 square feet (2,044 square meters) of retail space that Wieden selectively leases out, most recently, to a design store.

When Wieden + Kennedy and PICA moved in together, there was the fear that employees would find the atmosphere intimidating with the art, the artists, and the newness of it all. The goal was not to make it a hushed shrine to the arts, but to make it a factory full of noisy, wild creatives. Always in the back of everyone's mind is that the building was once a factory, and still is, a factory to produce ideas.

By moving Wieden + Kennedy into its new home, Wieden believes he's created new sources of inspiration for his employees. Employees are treated to PICA-hosted artists-in-residence, like the Bebe Miller Dance Company, when the troupe practiced for its show in the amphitheater during work hours. Author and illustrator Art Spiegelman and radio host Ira Glass are invited for lunchtime discussions. Wieden also hopes the agency's presence in the neighborhood and its collaboration with PICA will help nurture the community's interest in creativity and the arts.

Individual photos of the entire staff are displayed on the stairwell to celebrate Wieden + Kennedy's engine of creativity. The gallery-like atmosphere of the space pays homage to the individuals who work there, not to prior awards or old works and campaigns. The gallery is more about living in the present than the past.

"I have always had this dream in which people in our business could work alongside artists."

Dan Wieden, co-founder of Wieden + Kennedy

Lots of homey touches warm up the office/museum. Sofas and chairs with a lived-in look are found in many nooks and crannies around the building. Everyone takes advantage of the three beer dispensers that are parked around the building, and the hammock on the roof deck. In the workspaces, people work at 10-foot-long (3-meter-long) wooden tables rather than on standard office desks. Small seating areas that are bound by railings, but open, invite privacy and collaboration all at once.

The amphitheater is multipurpose. Wieden + Kennedy wanted to fix the problem of growing bureaucracy in the company. In the old space, it was too difficult to bring everyone together for a meeting at a moment's notice. Built into the new headquarters, a soaring atrium with the amphitheater is the core of the building, a gathering place. The four-story amphitheater holds the entire company for meetings, and also fills up during the day with working artists, writers, dancers, and performance artists, all in the spirit of collaborative creativity. Hundreds of people regularly attend shows after hours and on weekends; many visitors make themselves at home in the amphitheater.

"Overly hierarchical corporate rules about space can drive a stake between you and your plans to innovate." Tom Kelley, IDEO and author of *The Art of Innovation*

The bank of workstations seen in the photo at right is set up for freelancers and drop-in visitors. It can be found directly behind the reception area (above). Strands of seemingly different colors are expertly threaded throughout the space in a three-dimensional way by tying together wall and upholstery. If various hues were used on the walls only with banks of singular colored chairs, the effect would be flat and confusing to the eye at the same time. The lightweight purple and straw club-like chairs are imported from the Philippines.

COLOR MY WORLD
LUMINA AMERICAS INC.

Lumina, a company that specializes in marketing projects and products to the Latin American populations, started out as a dot.com and incubator company for smaller start-ups. Now, the company has one Web-based company, but in general, the company specializes in promoting Latin culture globally.

Lumina began to grow in size at the turn of the century—a time when premium commercial office space was scarce in Manhattan. Luckily, they found a space in an old loft building in NoHo, or North of Houston Street in lower Manhattan. The 14,000-square-foot (1,300-square-meter) space was a maze, a borough of tiny little boxes in the form of cubicles and offices, says architect Heather Faulding of Faulding Architecture, a New York architectural and design firm. But both the architect and client saw the potential when they spotted the Corinthian columns throughout the space. Demolition began immediately, save for those columns, and the end result of custom-designed workstations and handpicked furniture comfortably fits over 100 people.

A WELCOME SPACE

From the start, the client wanted anyone coming into the space to be welcomed, included, and immediately involved in what was going on in the company. "It was imperative that the space conveyed the spirit of the company as soon as anyone walked in," Faulding says.

That meant leaving open space under the brick arches, but also lots of meeting rooms and a cafeteria. The client wanted to veer away from the dot.com look of the day and create an identity that was clear, serious, elegant, yet fun and young at the same time. Faulding explained to the client her philosophy of creating a solid corporate culture. "I told them that if they wanted to do an open plan, it will only work if everyone sits in an open plan, except for the three directors of the company," Faulding says. "I believe that if you start to give middle managers private offices instead of larger workstations, trouble begins in the form of hierarchy."

A TWIST ON SERIOUSNESS

It remained that the three directors had private offices while the rest of the space was open plan. The three directors' offices are different, fresh, and as colorful as the rest of the space, but with an edge of seriousness. "There are huge financial decisions that are made in these offices, and they did not want anything crazy," Faulding says. "So, we tweaked the seriousness a bit by adding color."

Walls in the private offices are a cherry red, softened by the subdued chalkiness of the brick walls, honey-colored wood floors, and huge arched windows. Conference rooms are painted blue, yellow, or apple green. And every task chair is a different color, as well. "People are so afraid of color," Faulding says. "It's safe to do white walls and pale upholstery, but Lumina likes to take risks so we opened the floor up with color that flows from one space to the next."

"More people need to feel free to create a work environment that keeps everyone happy and lively." Heather Faulding, architect

David Perez, founder and president of Lumina Americas Inc., decided to create a sitting and meeting area under the arch in his office. Architect Heather Faulding encouraged him to set up a gallery of photos he took while on his travels. "I want more people to bring the soul of themselves into their office space," Faulding says. Bob Barocci, chief operating officer, set up his corner private office so he looks out into the open plan through glass walls that are glazed waist down, clear on top.

Peter Davidson, Lumina's chief executive officer who makes financial decisions for the company, preferred to be tucked away under an arch in a small alcove near a window. That way, he would not feel so out in the open while working on sensitive documents, even in his private office. The side chair is upholstered in a fabric with a repeating dog motif.

"Basically, I no longer work for anything but the sensation I have while working."

Albert Giacometti, sculptor

A BUNGALOW BUILT FOR TWO
BUNGALOW HEAVEN STUDIO

Blandine Saint-Oyant, an artist, and Andy Reath, a university professor, bought a home with a detached garage in Pasadena's historic landmark Bungalow Heaven district. A neighborhood filled with simple homes that are characterized by low-pitched roofs and wide eaves, and home to many artists and other creative homeowners, Bungalow Heaven is a rare and mostly intact collection of over 800 homes built from the 1900s through the 1930s. Because the neighborhood has attained landmark status, a conservation plan group assists homeowners with plans for restoration, alteration, and additions so that the historical and architectural qualities of the district remain intact and preserved. The association prefers that homeowners keep the characteristic wide, wraparound porches with deep overhangs that provide restful shelter from the sun, natural ventilation with the use of many windows, an open floor plan, and minimal ornamentation. Any garage alterations are also under scrutiny by the association.

"It is the supreme art of the teacher to awaken joy in creative expression and knowledge." Albert Einstein, physicist

SHARING THE STUDIO

The local design firm of Clerkin & Clerkin was hired to transform an old two-car garage with broken siding into a work haven for the couple. Saint-Oyant needed a tall, light-infused space while Reath, who works at home part of the week, needed a bright, serene area for contemplation. The result is a shared, yet separate space that gives the couple privacy for contemplation and creativity. "I'm a philosophy professor, and as an academic, I spend a lot of time at my desk," Reath says. "The office provides me a space where I can concentrate, and I can work there without feeling enclosed or cut off from the outside."

Reath's office overlooks the landscaped area that surrounds the workspace. The desk is nestled under the large double window in the office, which overlooks the small garden area the couple continues to nurture.

The art studio is light infused. "What I find inspiring about my studio is that it is a simple and neutral structure with good wall space and good natural light from the skylights," Saint-Oyant says. "It's a quiet, private space, thirty steps away from our house, so that when ideas come, I am instantly there."

The renovated garage is simple in size and stature, keeping the Bungalow Heaven architecture intact by blending contemporary windows and building materials to shape unimposing, scaled-down architectural additions.

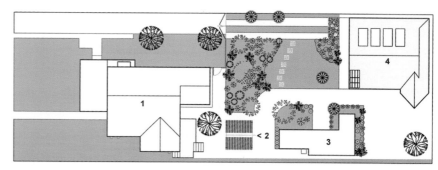

1. MAIN HOUSE   2. TRELLIS   3. GUEST HOUSE   4. STUDIO/HOUSE

Four-foot-wide (1.2-meter-wide) sliding doors lead into the artist studio. Doors needed to be wide to ventilate the oil painting studio. On sunny days, Saint-Oyant covers the doors with screening material that diffuses light. Two large windows high above the doors are low-budget translucent Plexiglas panels that shut out strong sun but let in more diffused daylight. The left side of the studio is higher to accommodate the artist's huge paintings.

Simplicity reigns in this sparsely furnished design studio. Three huge windows in the renovated chapel let in lots of daylight. Pull-down shades on the lower part of each window keep glare to a minimum. Additional vintage lights hang from the vaulted ceiling.

GOING TO THE CHAPEL

A ramshackle Victorian grammar school circa 1880 in London began its new life when owners Debbie and Nick Boon moved in. The schoolhouse sits on two acres, and includes an airy chapel with soaring ceilings framed in refurbished wood—a perfect spot/artist's studio for the couple's design business. Previous owners used the architecturally stunning chapel as a garage to service cars. Today, the freshly painted studio is sunny, bright, and used only to service a wayward light box or computer. The space is split into two rooms. A main work area is located in the high-vaulted chapel for creative work. A second area with pine table and upholstered chairs is fitting for casual meetings. There, Debbie, a full-time children's book author and illustrator, and Nick, an artist and designer, have merged their creative work lives.

"Just when ideas fail, a word comes in to save the situation."
Johann Wolfgang von Goethe, German poet, dramatist, novelist, and scientist

Architect Garth Rockcastle and sculptor and book designer Karen Wirth created the main public staircase. The staircase is a metaphor for a book, and looks like the spine of a book. It unfolds step by step as a book does page by page. Next to the stair is the café, where part of the building's original tin ceiling hangs.

POETIC JUSTICE
OPEN BOOK

Open Book, a project for a new literary and book arts center, is the result of a collaboration of three established independent arts organizations: the Minnesota Center for Book Arts, The Loft, and Milkweed Editions. Each nonprofit organization lived elsewhere until it became clear that by co-locating and interacting on a spontaneous basis, the result would be the exploration of collaborative opportunities and innovative programming to benefit the community at large.

Meyer, Scherer & Rockcastle (MS&R), the Minneapolis design firm, was brought in to help them find a suitable space and then turn the building into an expression of the arts, all on a rather limited budget. A 55,000-square-foot (5,110-square-meter) warehouse in a transitional neighborhood between the city's downtown and university area was developed into a thriving art center and workspace. The building is set in an ideal position, easily accessible to interstates and bus lines—anyone from any walk of life can visit the center.

KNITTING TOGETHER CONCEPTS

MS&R's Garth Rockcastle, principal in charge of the project, and Kate Berquist, project manager, were faced with a turn-of-the-century warehouse with various additions and four levels. The architects and designers set out to knit the building's components together rather than keep them separate in design and function. The challenge, however, was to design an interior that would be inviting, intriguing, and attractive to patrons of the arts from disparate income levels, but who are all passionate about and dedicated to literature. "This is an important consideration for all workspaces where people come from varying backgrounds," Rockcastle says. If they designed a high-end space specifically to attract wealthy patrons, then those of modest incomes wouldn't visit the building and the organizations would lose that important and vital energy. The goal was to open the building to everyone and anyone who has a love of literature.

UNCOVERING THE BUILDING'S SECRETS

The solution was to let the building speak to the designers and architects. It wasn't such an esoteric idea, the building had a lot to say. "We engaged the building in a conversation," Rockcastle says. "We uncovered and honored these traces of the building's history, then we edited the discoveries, left some repositories in time, and removed others."

The building began to open up and reveal its checkered history. Although it served as a warehouse for thirty years, there was something more joyous underneath the surface. The design program embraced the limitations of the budget and the realities of these turn-of-the-century buildings, while judiciously editing the lyrical composition and intervention of old and new. Framing, layering, and collaging of elements became the most effective (in budget and impact) to relate the found elements with the invented and to infiltrate the remembered with the imagined. MS&R worked to avoid cliché and superficiality to create spaces that a diverse community of writers, artists, and publishers would feel comfortable to visit and to use.

A PLAY ON WORDS

Several artists were invited to collaborate on the design of the elements, the most substantial being the central staircase. Together with a book artist, MS&R infused the intrinsic and compatible ideas of the book with the stair (sequential, transporting, revealing). Other artists helped to reinterpret and reuse some of the historic traces and to create unique furniture to help pique visitor and patron curiosities.

Since the renovation, this once-dismal area is being further developed. Two major cultural institutions have moved into this nearly abandoned section of town. The Guthrie Stage and the McPhale Center for the Arts joined Open Book to make this part of town the place in which art lovers now converge. The success of Open Book goes to show that neglected and worn structures are often devalued and decommissioned, and waiting for demolition when they would rather be discovered and turned into a poetic surprise.

"Whether we are poets or parents or teachers or artists or gardeners, we must start where we are and use what we have. In the process of creation and relationship, what seems mundane and trivial may show itself to be a holy, precious part of a pattern."

Luci Shaw, poet, essayist

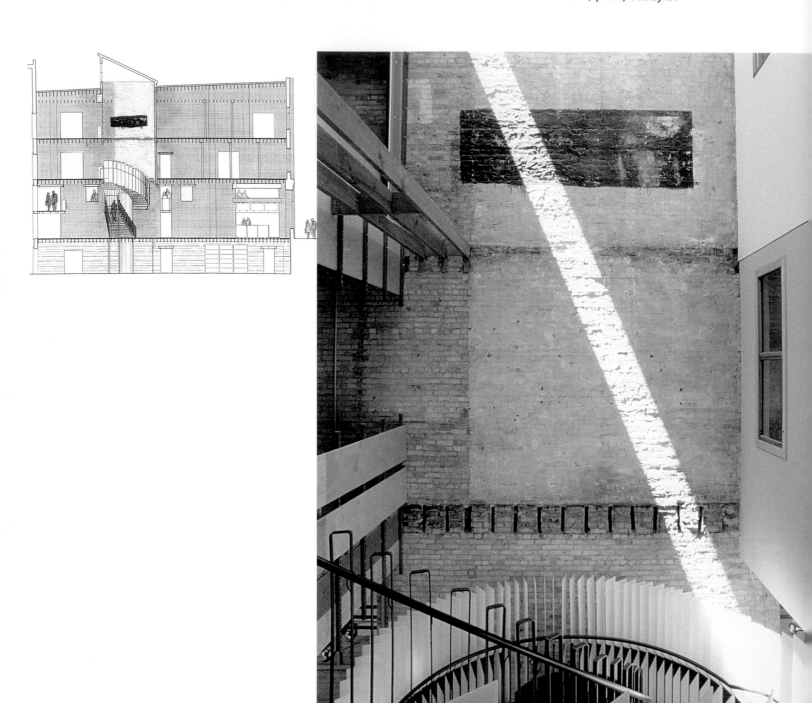

Interior windows were placed in the stairwells to offer visitors and employees glimpses of what people are working on without invading their privacy too much. Architect Garth Rockcastle says it's a way for diverse populations to observe and share with one another.

"If at first the idea is not absurd, then there is no hope for it."

Albert Einstein, physicist

Rather than remove the original staircase, it was shortened and left on the wall as a trace of the old building. Other fragments of history from the building were found and some were framed and placed in odd areas of the building to surprise and entertain visitors and employees. Rockcastle used the concept of *palimpsest*, which means leaving traces of history and occupation or use.

Huge original loading dock doors
painted a fresh green are used as
office and conference room dividers.

Artist Laura Migliorino became enamored with the building and developed a photo essay detailing some of the building's unearthed fragments. She created collages of the elements, such as wall covering from when the building was a hotel, and placed the artwork in unexpected parts of the building, such as in the back exit stairwell, in the janitor's closet, and anywhere someone would least expect to find a piece of art.

A brick wall with worn Polish script was left in this private office. The trace of history was left as a way to show visitors that the interior is an ongoing discovery of elements to the building's biography, much like that of reading a book.

GALLERY
FACES OF INSPIRED WORKPLACES

In the mid-1990s, *The Wall Street Journal* launched its series "Workspaces," which profiles people who have unique offices and working environments. Most of the people profiled are executives, but are managers with a twist. They are willing to weave their personal passions throughout their places of work. The result is a workspace that is personalized and inspired, a place that keeps them energized and productive, as well as bringing joy to employees. From a lawyer who dons jeans and prefers a rustic rather than refined tone to his office to a doctor who transformed his garage into an antique apothecary, these workspaces are represented by a group of people who aren't afraid to break free from a prescribed mold of what most people think a workspace should look like. Instead, they surround themselves with elements of their lives and personalities that help them get through stressful—but always inspired—days of creative work.

COMIC RETREAT
SERENE WORKSPACE
GABOR CSUPO, CO-CHAIRMAN, KLASKY CSUPO INC.

It takes a lot of work to create a runaway best-selling animated television program. But that's just what Gabor Csupo, co-chairman of Klasky Csupo, an animation company, did when he and his company dreamed up the Simpsons concept in 1988. The Rugrats movies began in 1999, thanks to the creative urges of Klasky Csupo, too. Who had been animator Gabor Csupo's greatest influences? Frank Zappa, controversial musician and friend, an inspiration that helped push him artistically to pioneer, challenge, and never imitate anything or anyone, always looking to surprise people with the unexpected. It's the philosophy behind Csupo's workspace, as well.

A colorful office, punctuated by the sinewy, plush sofa facing the wall of floor-to-ceiling windows, the space is at once playful and fantasy-like, and also soothing and quiet, despite the 9-foot (2.7-meter) shark hanging from the ceiling and sliding metal door next to the gong. The mix of grass green and beet red walls, blue and green sofa, watery blue glass bar, and berry–colored floor is Csupo's idea of the ultimate retreat. Anything monotone in color and square in shape could irk him; anything colorful, curvy, and quirky is loose and soothing. With all the diversions—including a tall rocket in the corner near the windows—there's much to relax with, as well. Along with near-to-his heart toys and a never-ending view, a stocked bar, library of joke books, and top-notch entertainment center in the office means Csupo doesn't have to go far to feel inspired.

WORKSPACE OF FAME
NURTURING WORKSPACE
JOHNNY GRANT, CHAIRMAN OF THE WALK OF FAME SELECTION COMMITTEE AND HONORARY MAYOR OF HOLLYWOOD

Legend has it that the term "honorary mayor" was coined in the 1920s by Hollywood press agents determined to create buzz for actors and films. The local chambers of commerce jumped on the concept, and named a few honorary mayors around the large city of Los Angeles, including Johnny Grant, dubbed head honcho of Hollywood, in recognition of his limitless civic work for his beloved community.

To this day, Grant remains honorary lifetime mayor of Hollywood, and since 1980, also chairman of the Walk of Fame selection committee. Grant, who has presided over hundreds of awards ceremonies and met and mingled with every celebrity to come through Hollywood's revolving door, has a collection of photos and mementos to show for it. Grant's home, and office, is a penthouse suite in the historic Hollywood Roosevelt Hotel where the Academy Awards were first presented. It's a home where memories have come to reside; Grant's walls are filled to the brim with framed photos of celebrity-studded events that he has attended.

His displays include cowboy-singer Gene Autry's rodeo saddle, comedian Bob Hope's golf clubs, and silent screen stars Mary Pickford and Douglas Fairbanks's old roulette table that Grant now uses as a desk. Grant, a radio and television host himself, likes to sit in a director's chair to do his work. The history of Hollywood, and the franchise he has helped to build with the name Hollywood, is alive and well and chronicled in Grant's workspace.

THERAPY ROOM
FANTASY WORKSPACE
EARL MINDELL, NUTRITIONIST, PHARMACIST, CONSULTANT, AND WRITER

Earl Mindell, R.Ph., Ph.D, took an ordinary garage and turned it into a workspace from another time and era, one that brings this nutritionist and pharmacist back to a world where more importance was placed on natural treatments than on man-made medicines.

Dr. Mindell, an expert on nutrition, drugs, vitamins, and herbal remedies, is also the author of a number of books, including *The Diet Bible*, *The Vitamin Bible for the 21st Century*, *Prescription Alternatives*, *Soy Miracle*, *Herb Bible*, *Anti-Aging Bible*, and *Peak Performance*. Dr. Mindell is also a registered pharmacist, master herbalist, and a professor of nutrition at Pacific Western University in Los Angeles. With that kind of pedigree resume, it's clear that Dr. Mindell's passion is the pursuit and perfection of past and present remedies for today's maladies.

His workspace is a tribute to the history of pharmacy; the shop is outfitted with turn-of-the-century architectural details, such as tin ceiling tiles and carved doors and molding that are backdrops for druggists' artifacts. There's a display of over 400 mortars and pestles, a variety of measuring scales, and a collection of hot-water bottles and handwritten pharmacy ledgers. Dr. Mindell keeps natural curatives throughout the workspace, including curative plants and prescriptive chalk from the 1800s. Even the restroom is outfitted with old-fashioned toiletries, and an old apothecary chest still smells of ether. Dr. Mindell has transformed the garage into a place where he feels most inspired to tinker and discover the exclusive nutrition formulations that has made him a success in the fickle world of diet and nutrition advice.

KID AT HEART
PLAYFUL WORKSPACE
JIM MCCAFFERTY, PRESIDENT AND CEO OF JMP CREATIVE

Jim McCafferty, president of JMP Creative, caters to marketing and product development people in the toy and film industry. But there's more to his playful workspace than shelves stocked with toys. The company, housed in a traditional industrial park, looks very plain from the outside. But McCafferty says he's worked hard to make the company's inside quarters as fun and exciting as possible for everyone that works there.

McCafferty has created a carnival-like atmosphere to keep everyone energized and surprised at every corner they turn. He stocks his shelves with displays and products his company has designed including Tekno, a robotic puppy that's become the prized pet of the twenty-first-century household. In addition, there are magic books and tricks, playbills, a slot machine filled with promotional buzzwords to stimulate creative thinking when the arm is pulled, plus a magic eight ball that in trying times will jog an answer to a problem. But there's even more than that to keep the creative juices flowing. There's the new 40-foot (12-meter) flying saucer built on a platform ten feet off the ground that holds thirty people, a place the staff uses for meetings, multi-media presentations, and brainstorming sessions. And don't be startled by life-like pirates scaling the walls around the company—McCafferty put them there to symbolize the employees' abilities to think in adventurous ways. There's a Fun House on the premises, too, with a 20-foot (6-meter) dinosaur, bumper cars, a giant fake monkey, and a 6-foot-long (1.8-meter-long) hot dog and a 5-foot-long (1.5-meter-long) lobster. The goal, says McCafferty, is to make the workplace wild, crazy, and fun.

"I like nonsense, it wakes up the brain cells. Fantasy is a necessary ingredient in living, it's a way of looking at life through the wrong end of a telescope. Which is what I do, and that enables you to laugh at life's realities." Theodore Suess Geisel, *aka* Dr. Seuss, author

"There's a fine line between genius and insanity. I have erased this line."
Oscar Levant, composer and actor

SHELTER FROM THE STORMS
SERENE WORKSPACE
LARRY FLYNT, PUBLISHER, LARRY FLYNT PUBLISHING, INC.

What would you expect to see in Larry Flynt's own office space? One would think that Larry Flynt, the charismatic, yet often controversial businessman and publisher, would revel in a flamboyantly designed office. Flynt's office is not exactly what you would have expected to find.

Behind the oval, black-glass Beverly Hills headquarters lays a den of antiquity, a shelter of serenity fit for the king of freedom of speech. Elegance reigns in this crusader's office. Persian rugs, lush velvet curtains, carved wood furniture, and reproductions of romantic paintings in ornate gill frames may shock the visitor, but it's a serene workspace for Flynt. Of course, there is *Sumo*, the Taschen book of Helmut Newton's photos, proudly sitting on a stand specially designed by Philippe Starck. It wouldn't be Flynt's office without just a tiny hint of skin.

LAW SUITE
SERENE WORKSPACE
MICHAEL GENDLER, GENDLER & KELLY

Michael Gendler, partner at Gendler & Kelly, is an attorney to actors, directors, and producers. As counsel to high-profile celebrities, one would expect to see Michael Gendler, partner, Gendler & Kelley, sitting in a pin-striped suit behind a carved mahogany desk. But, that's not so, says the faded jean-wearing attorney. Instead, Gendler is grateful and revels in the freedom he is afforded by working with creative clients. His wild and crazy clients, says Gendler, allow him the permission to express his authentic self in his own office space. His preferences: A clutter-free, sun-drenched workspace that lets him breathe.

Gendler's own office looks more like a downtown Manhattan loft with cement walls, exposed ceilings, and metal shelving, décor rarely found in law firms in the United States. Instead, Gendler prefers a desk of pine planks set on steel girders, vintage garbage cans, and old wood lawn chairs for client seating. To accessorize, Gendler likes austere black–and–white photos and drawings and iron desk trays. He'll also prefer to work standing at a steel drafting table that looks out to mountains. But to add warmth and comfort to the sunlit space, there's a Persian rug, aquarium, and a patina weathervane. Best of all, says Gendler, is the collection of gifts and souvenirs given to him by his own clients.

"If you are not living on the edge, you take up too much room."

Native American saying

SAFEGUARDING SPIRITS
ARTISTIC WORKSPACE
BOB MALONE, BRITISH PETROLEUM

Bob Malone, executive with British Petroleum PLC, a petroleum and petrochemicals company based in London, was faced with setting up an open office designed to encourage teamwork. His only wall—a bank of file cabinets separating him from his staff. His office is outfitted with the traditional elements of a wood desk, conference table, and sofa and chairs for casual meetings. What's different about this corporate office is the crew of kachina dolls that greet visitors to Malone's office. Malone's dolls aren't the kind your mother collects. A kachina doll is a sculptural art form that originated in the Hopi pueblo villages in northeastern Arizona. The figurines are hand carved from wood by Native American artists and represent the masked and costumed dancers of various spiritual aspects of life—sounds, animals, crops, earth, stars, moon and sun. The spirits are believed to visit the Hopi villages each year to bestow gifts of prosperity and luck to the townspeople. The dolls are an outgrowth of Malone's fascination with Native American art and culture, and he's able to express that passion by surrounding himself in his office with a collection of artifacts he's collected in his travels. Larry Hobbs, a master carver of Navajo ancestry, sculpts most of Malone's kachinas. Mixed among Hobbs's versions are antique dolls, as well. Malone has the right idea by surrounding himself and his staff with benevolent spirits.

DIRECTORY
PROJECTS AND DESIGNERS

PAGE 12
PROJECT/CLIENT: Mariposa
DESIGN FIRM: Olson Lewis & Dioli, 17 Elm Street, Manchester-by-the-Sea, MA 01944
TEL: 978-526-4386
www.oldarch.com

PAGE 18
PROJECT/CLIENT: Vitra
DESIGN FIRM: Sevil Peach Gence Associates, Nutmeg House, 60 Gainsford Street, London, SE1 2NY, UK
TEL: 0-20-7357-8656

PAGE 22
PROJECT/CLIENT: Westport Center
DESIGN FIRM: Gould Evans, 4041 Mill Street, Kansas City, MO 64111-3008
TEL: 816-931-6655
www.geaf.com

PAGE26
PROJECT/CLIENT: Campus MLC
DESIGN FIRM: Bligh Voller Nield, 189 Kent Street, Sydney, NSW2000, Australia
TEL: 612-9252-1222
www.bvn.com.au
PROJECT TEAM: Rosemary Kirkby, Debbie Berkhout, Jenny Fusca, Mark Zaglas; Architect: Bligh Voller Nield, James Grose

PAGE 32
PROJECT/CLIENT: Accenture
DESIGN FIRM: Marshall Cummings, 43 Davies Avenue, Toronto, ON, M4M 2A9, Canada
TEL: 416-461-3563
www.marshallcummings.com

PAGE 34
PROJECT/CLIENT: Orange Call Center (Nexus)
DESIGN FIRM: Nicholas Grimshaw & Partners, 1 Conway Street, Fitzroy Square, London W1T 6LR, UK
TEL: 0-20-7291-4141
www.ngrimshaw.co.uk
DESIGN TEAM: Richard Connor, Simon Dickens, Matthew Eastwood, Nicholas Grimshaw, Killian O'Sullivan, Stuart Piercy

PAGE 38
PROJECT/CLIENT: Herman Miller Senior Leadership Space
DESIGN FIRM: Meyer, Scherer & Rockcastle, 119 North 2nd Street, Minneapolis, MN 55401
TEL: 612-375-0336
www.msrltd.com
ARCHITECT: Paul Udris

PAGE 44
PROJECT/CLIENT: Studio at Third Avenue
DESIGN FIRM: Gould Evans, 3136 North 3rd Avenue, Phoenix, AZ 85013
TEL: 602-234-1140
www.geaf.com
OWNER OF VINTAGE AIRSTREAM: Paul Farley
farley@classicairstream.com

PAGE 52
PROJECT/CLIENT: CTV, Canada
DESIGN FIRM: Marshall Cummings, 43 Davies Avenue, Toronto, ON, M4M 2A9, Canada
TEL: 416-461-3563
www.marshallcummings.com

PAGE 54
PROJECT/CLIENT: Young & Rubicam
DESIGN FIRM: Haworth Ideation Group, One Haworth Center, Holland, MI 49423
TEL: 616-393-3000
www.haworth.com
HAWORTH IDEATION GROUP: Jeff Reuschel, Steve Beukema, Roque Corpuz, Ralph Reddig, Clarkson Thorp, Ronna Alexander, Jay Brand, Sally Augustin, Al Speet, Doug O'Kane, Ron Lamer
IDEA FACTORY DESIGNER: Arnold Wasserman

PAGE 56
PROJECT/CLIENT: Duffy Design & Fallon
DESIGN FIRM: MAP, 45 E. 20th Street, New York, NY 10003
TEL: 212-982-2020
www.ma.com

PAGE 62
PROJECT/CLIENT: Herman Miller Chicago Showroom
DESIGN FIRM: Krueck & Sexton, 221 West Erie Street, Chicago, IL 60610
TEL: 312-787-0056
Ayse Birsel, Olive 1:1, 589 8th Avenue, New York, NY 10018, 212-965-9001

PAGE 66
PROJECT/CLIENT: The Evans Group Headquarters
DESIGN FIRM: The Evans Group, 1001 North Orange Avenue, Orlando, FL 32810
TEL: 407-650-8770
www.theevansgroup.com
CONTRACTOR: Aagaard-Juergensen, 5695 Beggs Rd., Orlando, FL 32810, 407-298-1550
INTERIORS: Evcom, Division of The Evans Group

PAGE 72
PROJECT/CLIENT: Artist's Retreat
DESIGN FIRM: Henning Larsens Tegnestue, Vimmelskaftet 49, DK1161, Copenhagen, Denmark
TEL: 45-82-33-30-00
www.hlt.dk

PAGE 74
PROJECT/CLIENT: Essex Conference Center & Retreat, One Conomo Point Road, Essex, MA 01929
TEL: 978-768-7374
www.eccr.com

PAGE 78
PROJECT/CLIENT: Conference Barn
DESIGN FIRM: Sant Architects, 1601 Abbot Kinney Boulevard, Venice, CA 90291
TEL: 310-396-4828
www.santarchitects.com

PAGE 80
PROJECT/CLIENT: Meditation/Conference Room
ARTIST/DESIGNER: Stephen Hendee, 95-111 New Jersey Railroad Avenue, Newark, NJ 07105
TEL: 973-589-0166

PAGE 82
PROJECT/CLIENT: Triple 5 Soul
DESIGN FIRM: Qui Ly, Iota Office, 9-01 44th
Drive, Long Island City, NY 11101
TEL: 646-879-5005

PAGE 84
PROJECT/CLIENT: HBG New Media
DESIGN FIRM: Valerio Dewalt Train, 500 North
Dearborn Street, Chicago, IL 60610
TEL: 312-332-0363
www.vdtainc.com

PAGE 88
PROJECT/CLIENT: Dent Inc.
DESIGN FIRM: Austin Patterson Disston
Architects, 376 Pequot Avenue, Southport,
CT 06490
TEL: 203-255-4031
                          House of Fins, 99 Bruce
Park Avenue, Greenwich, CT 06830, 203-
661-8131
                    Jeanne Stoney Disston, Stoney
Disston Architects, 5 Garden Road, Weston,
CT 06883, 203-341-9995.

PAGE 92
PROJECT/CLIENT: Nexspace
DESIGN FIRM: Beckson Design Associates
933 North La Brea Avenue
Los Angeles, CA 90038
TEL: 323-874-6144
www.becksondesign.com

PAGE 96
PROJECT/CLIENT: Textile/Graphic Design Studio
DESIGN FIRM: Tow Studios, Peter Tow AIA, 59
Gansevoort Street, New York, NY 10014
TEL: 646-638-4760
www.towarchitecture.com

PAGE 102
PROJECT/CLIENT: Ringling Brothers
DESIGN FIRM: Faulding Architecture, 11 East
22nd Street, New York, NY 10010
TEL: 212-253-9172
www.f2inc.com

PAGE 104
PROJECT/CLIENT: Monster.com
DESIGN FIRM: Kahler Slater Architects, 111
W. Wisconsin Avenue, Milwaukee, WI 53203
TEL: 414-290-3734
www.kahlerslater.com

PAGE 106
PROJECT/CLIENT: PUSH
DESIGN FIRM: The Evans Group, 1001 North
Orange Avenue, Orlando, FL 32810
TEL: 407-650-8770
www.theevansgroup.com
CONTRACTOR: Aagaard-Juergensen, 5695
Beggs Rd., Orlando, FL 32810, 407-298-
1554
INTERIORS: Evcom, Division of The Evans
Group

PAGE 112
PROJECT/CLIENT: Cognex, One Vision Drive,
Natick, MA 01760
TEL: 508-650-3000
www.cognex.com

PAGE 114
PROJECT/CLIENT: Brendan Moore
DESIGN FIRM: Comley Van Brussel, 10 Four
Seasons Place, Toronto, Ontario M9B 6H7,
Canada
TEL: 416-621-7745
www.comleyvanbrussel.com

PAGE 118
PROJECT/CLIENT: Corey & Co., 63 Pleasant
Street, Watertown, MA 02472
TEL: 617-924-6050
www.corey.com

PAGE 122
PROJECT/CLIENT: Eric Roth's Barn, P.O. Box
422, Topsfield, MA 01983
TEL: 978-887-1975
www.ericroth.com

PAGE 126
PROJECT/CLIENT: David Pill Building
DESIGN FIRM: Pill Maharam Architects
TEL: 781-721-7604
www.pillmaharam.com

PAGE 128
PROJECT/CLIENT: Wieden + Kennedy
DESIGN FIRM: Allied Works Architecture,
2768 NW Thurman, Portland, OR 97210
TEL: 503-227-1737
www.alliedworks.com
PROJECT TEAM: Brad Cloepfil, Lorraine
Guthrie, Kyle Lommen, John Weil, Chris
Bixby, Jake Freauff, Jennifer Fowler, Jeff
Lee, Jody Lewis, Brian Malady, Doug
Skidmore

PAGE 134
PROJECT/CLIENT: Lumina Americas
DESIGN FIRM: Faulding Architecture, 11 East
22nd Street, New York, NY 10010
TEL: 212-253-9172
www.f2inc.com

PAGE 138
PROJECT/CLIENT: Bungalow Heaven
DESIGN FIRM: Clerkin & Clerkin, 1005 East
Colorado Boulevard, Pasedena, CA 91106
TEL: 626-568-3544
www.clerkin.com

PAGE 140
PROJECT/CLIENT: Open Book
DESIGN FIRM: Meyer, Scherer & Rockcastle,
119 North 2nd Street, Minneapolis, MN
55401
TEL: 612-375-0336
www.msrltd.com

DIRECTORY
PHOTOGRAPHERS

James Bedford/www.jamesbedford.com: 35, 36, 37

Björg Photography: 96, 97, 98 (top right & left, bottom), 99 (left)

Anthony Browell/Bligh Voller Nield Pty. Ltd., Architect: 26 (left & right), 27, 28, 29

Bligh Voller Nield Pty. Ltd., Architect: 30, 31

Amos Chan/Lori Weitzner Textiles: 99 (right)

Frederick Charles/Faulding Architecture, Inc.: 102, 103

Comley Van Brussel Design + Management: 115

Dan Cornish/Austin Patterson Disston Architects: 89, 90 (top & bottom), 91

Marshall Cummings: 32, 33 (top & bottom), 52 (top & bottom), 53

The Evans Group: 68 (bottom)

Stephen Gersh: 74, 75, 76, 77

Courtesy of The Glidden Company: 120

Benjamin Harris, b.s.k.: 82 (top, bottom left & right), 83

Haworth, Inc.: 54 (top), 55 (left)

Haworth/Steven Micros, Microsfoto: 54 (bottom & right), 55 (top right & bottom)

Bob Heimstra: 81

Stephen Hendee: 80

Steve Hall/©Hedrich Blessing: 42; 62, 64 (top left, right & bottom) 65 (left & right)

Roger Hill/Photosphere Studio: 38 (top), 38 (bottom left & right), 40, 41

Courtesy of Ikea Home Furnishings: 8, 25

Courtesy of Izzy Design: 71

Jens Lindhe/Henning Larsen Tegnestue A/S: 72, 73 (left & right)

Karant & Associates, Inc.: 84, 86, 87

©Douglas Keister: 47 (right)

Andrew Lautman/Monticello: 24

Mark Samuel Lee: 111 (right)

©John Edward Linden: 78, 79 (top & bottom), 92, 93, 94 (left & right), 95

MAP: 56

Laura E. Migliorino, Artist: 144

Olson, Lewis, & Dioli Architects: page 14

Stuart O'Sullivan/Faulding Architecture, Inc.: 134, 135 (left & right), 136, 157

Faulding Architecture (floor plan): 138

Raffi Alexander/www.spiderbox.com: 147, 148, 149, 151, 152, 154, 155

Ben Rahn Design Archive: 114, 116 (left & right), 117

Courtesy of Brendan Moore & Associates: 115

Ramesch Amruth/Vitra: 18, 19 (top), 20 (top & bottom), 21

©Eric Roth: 13, 15 (left & right), 16, 122, 123, 124 (left), 125 (left & right), 126, 127 (top left, right & bottom)

Sevil Peach: 19 (bottom)

©Rick Sferra: 140, 142 (right), 143, 145 (left & right)

Meyer, Scherer & Rockcastle: 142 (left)

Mike Sinclair/Gould Evans: 22 (left & right), 23

Sally Schoolmaster/Wieden + Kennedy: 128, 129, 131, 132 (left & right), 133

Courtesy of Steelcase, Inc.: 10

Frederick R. Stocker: 138 (bottom), 139 (top)

©Laurence Taylor: 66, 67, 68 (left & right), 69 (top & bottom)

Push: 106, 108, 109, 110 (top left, right & bottom), 111 (left)

Bill Timmerman/Gould Evans: 44, 45, 46 (left), 46 (right), 47 (left)

©Paul Warchol Photography Inc.: 57, 58, 59, 60, 61 (left & right)

www.elizabethwhiting.com: 48, 49, 50, 51, 139 (bottom)

Brian Wilder: 101; 105 (left & right), 113; 118 (left, middle & right)

Francine Zaslow: 12, 17

THE AUTHOR

Marilyn Zelinsky is one of the nation's leading experts on workplace design. Zelinsky is the former senior editor of *Interiors Magazine* and was a contributing author for *Corporate Interiors II*. She's also written extensively on residential interior design. Articles by and about Zelinsky have appeared in hundreds of publications, including *Business Week*, *USA Today*, *PC Magazine*, *This Old House*, *I.D.*, *ASID Icon*, *Today's Facility Manager*, *HomeStyle Magazine*, *Woman's Day Special Interest Publications*, *Family Circle*, *Home Office Computing Magazine*, *Home Furnishings News*, and a number of Meredith Corporation publications including *The Great American Kitchen Magazine*. Zelinsky is also a frequent guest on national television news and radio programs to discuss workplace design issues.

Also by Marilyn Zelinsky: *New Workplaces for New Workstyles*
                                   Practical Home Office Solutions

ACKNOWLEDGMENTS

I would like to thank all of the patient and gracious photographers and designers I worked with to create this timely and unique book. I'd especially like to thank editors Paula Munier, Betsy Gammons, Wendy Simard, and Nora Greer for their direction and composure. And last but not least, I'd like to thank William Speake of The Art of Working in Oakville, Ontario, for leading me to Canada's inspired workspaces.